STARBRIGHT - STARLIGHT

Anna Daniel

BALBOA.
PRESS

A DIVISION OF HAY HOUSE

Balboa Press books may be ordered through booksellers or by contacting:

Balboa Press
A Division of Hay House
1663 Liberty Drive
Bloomington, IN 47403
www.balboapress.com.au
1 (877) 407-4847

Because of the dynamic nature of the Internet, any web addresses or links contained in this book may have changed since publication and may no longer be valid. The views expressed in this work are solely those of the author and do not necessarily reflect the views of the publisher, and the publisher hereby disclaims any responsibility for them.

The author of this book does not dispense medical advice or prescribe the use of any technique as a form of treatment for physical, emotional, or medical problems without the advice of a physician, either directly or indirectly. The intent of the author is only to offer information of a general nature to help you in your quest for emotional and spiritual well-being. In the event you use any of the information in this book for yourself, which is your constitutional right, the author and the publisher assume no responsibility for your actions.

Any people depicted in stock imagery provided by Thinkstock are models, and such images are being used for illustrative purposes only.
Certain stock imagery © Thinkstock.

Printed in the United States of America.

ISBN: 978-1-4525-2675-1 (sc)
ISBN: 978-1-4525-2676-8 (e)

Balboa Press rev. date: 12/09/2014

INTRODUCTION

This book has been written to help guide and lighten the way for the many searching souls. It has been a great help to myself and so I hope it will be to many other genuine souls that are looking for a connection and a way to understand what life is all about. Anarama has been my main teacher from within my big team and therefore is credited for each reading – TttA, The truth through Anarama.

I also wish to thank Kevin for his editing and technical assistance and Noel and Jamie for their proof reading and support. A big thank you to all teachers, masters and healers that have aided me to complete this book.

This book could also be used to be opened at random to get a message from the source.

Love and light to all readers from the source

Anna.

CALM AND JOYFUL!

Let these two words give you what you want. Go ahead, relax and recharge, you have to keep your energy levels up for the times to come. Try not to look too far ahead at this stage, there will be help and support for you, so just take one day at a time. When you finally get organized, try to stay organized, it will just help you to clarify what is next on your agenda. The same old principles will apply with old wisdom's and old habits having to be separated; old habits particularly, because they tend to stay around just because you are so used to them or because they allow you to not have to think. Have a look at some of them today and ask yourself could some of them be replaced or changed altogether.

Always yours in eternal love. TttA.

PEACE TO ALL!

Let my peace and harmony stay with you forever, you are going through a time of change at the moment so try to go with the flow. There is no point at all in trying to stay behind or even sitting on the fence for a while, that just comes back to stagnation again. Resting for a while is good if you feel you have too but don't get used to it, it could become a habit, fresh winds in your sail will do far more to recharge you. Go ahead with your daily plans that we have given you, endurance is very important now so stay strong and don't get too involved in other things. Nature will give you what you need, just wait and listen, we will not give you more than you can handle for any one day.

Love eternal from all of us. TttA.

CO-OPERATE!

We know that you intend too but sometimes you just get your work tasks in the wrong order. Discipline is needed and it does count so keep up with your work. At present there are many changes in front of you and the timing is all out, as you put it, but that's because everything here where we are is under reconstruction. This is what we meant when we said "a new heaven and a new Earth". Many have tried to interpret these words but they all made one mistake. You must ask us first. Don't you make the same mistake and don't try to put your own interpretation on them to suit your own needs.

Just keep on listening in. TttA.

ONCE AGAIN - ONE DAY AT A TIME!

Let us do the organizing, don't think that you on your own know enough, some people think they can always tell but that isn't so, not without checking with us first. At these times you should be careful not to make assumptions. Your life is changing so rapidly, so how could you know. Most people rely on their ego but that's not good for the higher self. Be aware Children of the Light; now is your testing time, how far can you go without stumbling or taking the wrong turn on your path? When we say no it means just that. By acting too soon you could ruin months of good work so stay close, be clear and alert.

Lots of loving thoughts from us. TttA.

PREPARE!

Make sure you follow through on our guidelines, we are concerned about the slackness of some and the way they think it won't happen. Well that's up to them, all you can do is try to warn them and get them to look at their life. Try to let go a little more of personal situations, they're not your problems and you can only do what's on your plate. If they don't listen, stop giving them messages. The wedding from so long ago followed the same sort of pattern, so just be ready to change and draw your lines when the situation calls for it.

Withdraw and recharge. TttA.

DAWN GREETINGS!

Once again you have gone even deeper to meet me for wisdom and strength. To be able to see, hear and feel is of the most value today but don't be so sure that you know about what's going on, the ego should not be allowed to rise above the higher self. You need to understand that this is a priority for you. Development, the ability to understand and to evolve is your path, so try to detach, go forward and you will conquer and advance. Life is not really what it always seems to be, look under the masks and covers, believe in magic and magic will happen. Straying from your path will not be to your advantage, it'll just take up more of your time and energy.

More tomorrow for you, love from us all. TttA.

LET GO AND LET IT FLOW!

Remember what I said and follow through, always keep thinking about what is best for the development of your goal. The only thing you can take with you when one day you go is wisdom and the growth of your spirit. The third dimension still holds a lot of resentment and sorrows, sometimes even anger, unfortunately dealing with it the wrong way leads to the destruction of your spirit growth. That always happens when you use your energy to rid yourself of those feelings, sort things out before you bury them deep inside for years. Forgive and put yourself in the other persons shoes, there is always a reason for the other person's actions. Love comes from forgiveness. Smile a little more and again I say – 'one day at a time'.

Love from us. TttA.

MAINTENANCE!

To practice maintenance is to care and to want to make things last. Nurturing is another way to revitalise yourself and others. Today's meeting with us gave you some more connections and later on when you did your communication with others that came across. That's how we will work with you, just pass on what we give you, we need you as our anchor on Earth and at the same time we will train you to listen in and to be vigilant. Remember to wash your hands and to drink a lot of water after each case you deal with. That will keep you clean so that you don't get any contamination in your own system. Keep going and we will give you more work.

Blessings to you from us through A and CJ.

PRAISE BE!

Let no one hinder you with adversity or any other form of interference. We know how many times you have been tested and tried, we know you have had so many trying to alter you in one way or another but it did not happen and because of that you will know what's going on most times. Persevere and try to stay calm in all kinds of weather, if you don't your energy levels will drop. You are going to need all of it in the future, to act as an anchor is one thing, to be one is another thing. Ponder this truth and give it a chance to enlighten you.

Blessings my dearest. TttA.

THERE IS A PLACE FOR
EVERYTHING AND EVERYONE!

Remember what we advise you, everyone has their part to play and you can be sure the big puzzle is operating. You should not query who and why some people do what you might think is illegal or unacceptable, that's nothing to do with you, stick to your path and see things for what they are. Don't you start to use others for the wrong motive, always be honest and act without fear. Don't think that you have to be perfect, people that operate on that level often get exhausted or waste time, what's really important is the way your soul progresses so try to spend most of your time, energy and love on spiritual growth. Pass that message on, it's not your responsibility as to how they take it or what the outcome of it is. We will take care of that.

Love always. TttA.

MORE DISCIPLINE!

Get your priorities in order, to get carried away doing unimportant things serves no purpose. Start afresh each morning and because you will be very busy later on, try and do your connections before you get up. Stay organized and let us sort out your day. If you think it should be after your head visions you are mistaken. Don't ever think that you know it all, remember that the spirit is in charge and that everything comes from the source, so stay steady and calm and you will advance much faster. Time is speeding up so things will be a bit unbalanced for a while but be patient and only act when we say so.

So many people are involved in your life so you need to remember our teachings. TttA.

NEW PATTERN!

Let my spirit flow through you and always come to the source for your guidance. Show others what their path can hold and how it can unite and support them in these times. You all have different gifts so put them all together and miracles will happen. Just be aware and listen carefully, sing a new song, gone are the days of old. When you do release old patterns leave them alone, otherwise how else can you start afresh? It all takes time; to not fall into traps, to recognize what is going on and to learn to follow through. Just relax and enjoy things once again. The danger is in getting used to one way of living and not thinking. Have a fresh day.

Love from the team. TttA.

JOY FOREVER MORE!

Let it be and always try to find a course that can be celebrated, don't be too hasty but by all means follow through and try to keep going ahead. The weather will influence you and your pets but that is because you are so sensitive to the changes in the air and temperature. The ones that feel and see a lot can always pick up the changes in the atmosphere so just try to go along with it one day at a time and try to stay positive at all costs. Yesterday was another day when too many people got carried away, for your part, try to stay in the middle and you will always have enough.

Love as always. TttA.

LET IT FLOW!

Let life flow around you if you want to have a really healthy life, stagnant waters are not good for your growth. You have almost let go of your disbeliefs and the things that cause you to stumble and that's good because they will only block up the 'river'. Believe and tell yourself that you are perfect in spirit, mind, body and emotion and always try to let your spirit come first. At the same time go ahead and sort out what you want sorted out in your life. Look to see how you feel after each person has left after a sitting or a visit and if you feel any unease or sadness ask us and we will clear it, but watch out the next time a return connection is in place. Let our light and love penetrate your whole being, right to your very core. Those that come for a sitting or a visit will benefit from it, especially the many who are so very hungry for the universal truth.

Blessings and love to you. TttA.

LET ME WORK THROUGH YOU!

Be willing to be a channel, to work for the light and of course for the enlightenment for human kind. Don't see yourself as a separate entity that has to be isolated and completely detached from the third dimension, rather that you need to be in it to be able to operate and to understand what is going on. The people in the third dimension are mostly controlled by the media or mass hypnosis and therefore detached from the greater spirit, and because you now know that you have to take that into consideration when dealing with them. Ask them about where they are and where they are going and if they don't know and are fogged in, let us clear the fog and inform you how to deal with them.

Love as always. TttA.

REJOICE!

Rejoice at all times and for every situation. All happenings occur to let you know what you have to learn and what you have to look at, meanwhile we will be standing by and keeping a close watch over you until the end of the year. One of your tasks at the moment is to be aware and to listen, you need to stay firm and to be steadfast, to act as an anchor. Don't waver, we fully understand how hard it can be for you sometimes, but hang in there. Things are indeed at a breaking point and you must decide who you are working for, there can be no more grey areas – undecided entities do not serve anyone's purpose. Try to go forward in the name of the light.

Blessings from all of us. TttA

RELAX MORE!

You can't do any of your tasks when you are so tense, so trust us to give you ways to relax so that you can get on and operate properly. Each morning when you wake, or before you go to sleep in the evening, if you surrender your will to us we will give you ways to totally relax and to enjoy moments of pure earthly pleasure. Enjoy these times and know that we are recharging you so that you can go forward. Lives are slowly being sorted out, some are getting more tangled but others are gradually clearing things up and in reality it just means change for everyone, just where is up to you. To take a stand and to know where you belong in the scheme of things is of the upmost importance, so work on your buffer zone, it must be stronger so that you can operate in a good fashion. Take notice of who is organized now and who wants to do something about it, support the ones that are trying and let go of the rest. That shouldn't be too hard to do, just set up your boundaries and don't forget to have an exchange.

Lots of support and love from us all. TttA

START AGAIN!

Look at what you have, not what you don't have and work on what you want and can achieve with our help. Send out love and eternal light in bigger measures and because it's a trying time at present go easy on yourself. Keep putting out requests and stay positive, you will in time get used to the new thought patterns that we are giving you. Gone are the old times, enough is enough, start to live and let things unfold. It will go slowly at first but it will evolve. The keeper must understand he has to look at his own situation very clearly and that it is not your problem. You need more of a demonstration of life from him and sympathy will only delay this. In a crisis time it is okay to be sympathetic but not all of the time, most of the time it is just a habit.

Cheer up; love from us all. TttA.

REJOICE!

Let someone know and feel your heavenly joy. The world's change is under activation and the more cheer and joy that you give out the better the shift will go. Only positive actions and thoughts will activate the move. Praise is another thing that you could emphasis but be aware who you mix with, send out your light and love in bigger measures. Today's walk and the work you did in the mall was very good for you, more of it will come, just go where the inspiration leads you, we will go with you. We are leading you but you must pass on to others what we give you and lead them.

Many blessings and much laughter to you. TttA.

REJOICE ONCE MORE!

Yesterday was the start of a closer connection with us and the more you can empty out the faster we can get you activated. The fourth dimension has been brought forward because of your time in eternity; the big move is really happening. Be aware of negativity, if you get slack or start to take things for granted you will easily be misled, so remember to be disciplined. Your best time is early in the morning when you have come back from us, keep on going and we mean in both ways. Let us be in charge and surrender to us every 24 hours. That's enough for anyone to deal with especially as the bigger picture is beginning to show. Thank you for your input.

Love as always. TttA.

WELL NOW!

You certainly have been busy but try not to be engaged in so many things at once. You need to concentrate and focus a little more. Life at present is confusing enough so stay alert, straight and try to be a little more emotionally detached. Emotional exchanges are okay as that's how you learn to understand what's going on but the subject does need to be looked into. It's normal for you to express your feelings when you want to, kept inside they could cause health problems later on, being yourself is natural to you unfortunately no one else seems to know that that's how you operate. You need to make it clear what's on the agenda but just don't use too many words, send the thought instead.

Lots of love and support. TttA.

JOY AND ETERNAL LAUGHTER!

It's what the world needs at the moment so you should all look into that area. You will need all the help you can get to shift the vibrations and to get them to go further out into the atmosphere. Your solar system is still under review and time is of the essence so try to keep spiritually, mentally and physically fit. The better you feel and act the better you can handle the transformation. Sometimes you get bogged down in Earthly life so try to stand back and don't let others' woes concern you so much. Today's happening will clear a little bit off the decks for you, so try to get out and let the beauty of nature heal you some more. We wish you health, wealth and reality today.

Love TttA.

LET LOVE AND JOY FLOW INTO YOU AND FROM YOU!

Be aware of sad and sick people at these times and try to let go of all your own problems. Mother Nature is your best healer; so much life and energy flows from your garden so try to get out into it. Look, listen and laugh out there but don't be discouraged if nothing visible appears, just keep going. Life is about to unfold for you so try not to go back to old patterns. You deserve the very best in life and after all your experiences you will come out on top, without any of the practical lessons you have had, you would not understand the courage and wisdom from al of us.

Love TttA.

RELAX AND REJOICE!

First of all before you can get more input from us and be refilled for further work and be able to heal yourself you must relax and empty out. Stay disciplined and rest when you are weary, your body will always tell you a story so listen to it. Any feelings that do not come out or are just talked about will get inside you and will leave you with an adverse disempowered condition. When or if you don't know what to do just wait, don't accept anything or anyone that will degrade, depress or devastate you. You also have to watch out for drama and discord. You are doing your best most of the time but because of other 'suckers' you are inclined to compare things with other situations from the past. Don't. Onwards and upwards.

Always yours. TttA.

PEACE OF MIND!

Let my peace flow into your whole being, not just a part of it and enjoy your freedom when you can. Some people think they have you worked out but little do they know, just leave it all behind you and try to grow from there. Today is a 'showing' day, most people do not like to be exposed but sooner or later it has to happen. Beforehand try to mix with as many positive people as you can, as in time they will give you the energy to be able to detach yourself from these days faster. Some wont go too far, others will, but that is okay, to have some boundaries is healthy and if more people had them the world would be an easier place to live in. After the 'showing' is over try to relax and restore yourself for the rest of the day.

We are with you and send you our love and support. TttA.

HEALING SOUNDS AND LIGHT!

The sounds of heavenly music and the light from the source will help your healing, if only everyone knew what a miracle it is going to be. Your words today, are so far removed from your old beliefs and what used to renew so many of them, yet the same formula is still there, so use it. Your mind must be at peace and your spirit centered in you, that's the most helpful way to get good input from us, so relax and enjoy today. Your life is unfolding, just as there are many changes going on in other peoples lives at present, so when you don't get any clear answers from us just wait. It's hard for some people but very wise generally. Your pets will also feel the changes so be patient. We will be with you, as always.

Love and wisdom from us. TttA.

FOCUS!

You did well today so try to stay focused like that and you will get more out of life, especially when you stop splitting up your good energy. You also need to understand that it's vital that you follow through and then withdraw. We sent you another reminder that we think you are doing your job, so just believe and let us do our work through you. Your blueprint is in order but still you must surrender every day, there is more work to come your way. Being involved is healthy and an exchange is taking place so lets have no more stale energy. God bless you and we all wish you courage.

Starbright, starlight. TttA.

LOOK AND LISTEN!

Most people see but really they don't know what's going on, the things that are most obvious at first glance are not necessarily what we want you to look at. Take the masks off some subjects, peel back some of the layers and surprise! Surprise! Disguises can be useful at times but don't overdo them, use them and the other practical advice we give you as a tool only if your safety is at risk. They are free and can be very powerful. Go ahead today and we will present you with new opportunities, don't concern yourself with odd feelings, people or the weather. It's all in the making today, so be patient and bear with us a little longer. Today is a gift, so that's why we call it a present.

Lots of love and laughter from all of us. TttA.

ENJOY AND RESTORE!

Believe the source one hundred percent and if you do happen to doubt for a second stop and connect with us. At the present time we are relying on our Earthly connections to do their part so there is a lot at stake, the timing is crucial. At times it wont appear to be but don't be fooled and remember at the end of the day to hand back to us that that is not finished, it is too much for you to carry it with you through the night. You can not recharge properly if you are already full of other things. Remember to go outside from time to time, nature will rest your weary spirit and tell you when it is at peace. Let it dwell within you and be centered.

Focus on that and learn how to stay centered. TttA.

REMEMBER!

You are so occupied at times but you will get back to a routine, to clear an area is to clear your mind, so don't clutter things up if you can help it. Keep your life in order, it's hard at times we know but take time out and try to be practical. Collecting specimens in the same area will strengthen and force you to understand the different energies, if you think back, you will remember. Keep writing and spending time with us, it's a basic, simple rule but it'll get you there quicker. Relax when you need to but don't waste time by getting into a pattern of putting things off. Stay focused on your priorities and leave the rest till the next day, keep doing your part.

Enjoy things, stay patient and listen in to us. TttA.

DELIGHT IN THE LIFE!

Try to be a better advocate for us, let others be as miserable as they wish to be, just don't you get involved in all their depressing situations. Stay smiling and take one day at a time. There are a lot of jumbled up people and situations out there today and they will try to take you down with them. It's a sign that they have a jumbled up master and it's so transparent what their training has been and who has taught them. You will need to ask yourself "Are you being used again or are you evolving with your eternal teaching?" Open your spirit to the light and still your mind so that the spirit can show itself for what's really there.

Love and blessings from all of us. TttA.

AGAIN YOU HAVE LOST
YOURSELF IN TIME!

Try harder to discipline yourself, there is so much going on at the moment however things will get better. Let my light guide you and show you the way so that you will know what door to enter through. Take note of who is entering your door, as it could be that it is someone that will not benefit you, rather they might just want to use you. Try shifting your guardian and see or take note of the response. Today is so sunny so try to enjoy it. It can and will benefit your whole physical being so shelve your 'hang-ups' and go out in it. Let it shine upon your complete earthly form. Make your day better by having fun with the little things. Let things come to you, just relax, smile and lose yourself in time for a while. It is okay.

Courage and laughter from all of us, especially me. TttA.

LET GO!

Follow through and let go of the last tangles, then and only then will you be free of "if's and but's" and you will have more energy. Yesterday's time of unrestrained indulgence, relaxation and gathering energy for your earthly body was a good example of the kind of freedom that we want you to pursue. 'Hang-ups' need to be a thing of the past. There will always be more from us but you must do your bit – co-operation is the word for today. Stay positive, mix with positive people and energies. Your system picks up too much sometimes so at times you must stay clear of certain lives in your dimension. The secluded life you have at the moment will only be temporary, when you get stronger you will mix more, still, be aware of leech's and 'scrambled egg' type people.

Blessings and courage from all of us. TttA.

UPWARDS AND ONWARDS!

Keep going and remember to enjoy this life. There is much to celebrate about your present Earthly shape and form but you will need to show some people what that joy can be all about. Try to celebrate it and get them involved. Remember to check who you are doing this with as some come in disguises but generally most believers will be all right. Some will try to enter and immediately feed upon your good energy, in those cases it is sometimes better to tell them to get their own, directly from the source. Sometimes things can't go forward until they do their own work first, so you will need to allow yourself and others to 'live and let live'. That means you letting go of your own interests first, so that they can come to a celebration of their own, without feeding from you. Detach at those times and smile.

Lots of love from all of us. TtA.

ENJOY!

Today we will show you how much you can enjoy things, things that at certain times you did not used to enjoy. Try to let life flow and the many mysteries that you have up till now not understood will unfold. You might wonder why now but it had to be the right time and conditions before we could show you how and why. Get the little things done but at the same time understand that it's all a part of your picture. We have not been holding back, it was just that we needed you to be clear and wise enough to see and hear the knowledge, knowledge that you used to know so long ago. For now try to let go and remember that yesterday is gone.

Keep the good wisdoms and discard the ones you no longer want. TttA.

SILENT NIGHTS AND LEARNING NIGHTS!

It's all a part of your learning and discipline but you can now see why it's taking such a long time. For you to grasp a little of a big truth at one time needs the right moment but it will get easier as time goes by. When you can't see where to go, stand back, you can only work when you are at peace and are relaxed. Your strength comes from the source, you know very well that that is a truth so believe and watch it happen, the outcome will be much better than you had wished for. Go in peace and carry out your tasks with a glad heart. You represent me, your risen Lord.

I am always your loving, healing and teaching friend. TttA.

TEMPORARY SITUATIONS!

Start to think about what everything means and try not to get to attached to anything or anyone. As you probably know, most things are only temporary; it is only the spirit that survives and always lives on. The very essence of life is your spirit, so nurture it most of all but remember that your body, mind and emotions are also important because they are the 'coat' that houses your spirit. Again and again you will be reminded of the truth of life and what makes it eternal so listen to nature and enjoy a natural way of life, unpolluted and free. Transmute poisons to acceptable useful standards if necessary. More tomorrow.

Peace be with you. TttA.

TIME WARPS!

Don't delay the timing, we are there for you now, so try to drop some of your cares and believe that we love you. Know that we know how much you care and just how much you want to fulfill your pathway. Go ahead and enjoy your day and spread as much light around you as possible. Delight in the source and keep up the good work, laugh in the face of adversity and love things that come your way. It is the only way so don't delay, activate these things now and bridge the gap between people.

Blessings and love from all of us. TttA.

GLAD TIDINGS!

Go ahead and spread your good wishes and glad tidings. Good news comes when it is most wanted and today's plan will turn out to be an experience to remember. Stop your mind from wandering, stay in tune and stay healthy and alert – all will be well. Today's phone call will be deeper but until it comes keep sending out thoughts of love and abundance. It will come. Believe and understand that anything is possible in the name of light and love and just rejoice and trust that all is indeed well. Wonders are unfolding.

Lots of love and cheer from us all. TttA.

AGAIN AND AGAIN!

Time seems to just go by or is it speeding up? The big change is upon you and for some it's hard to understand why but as long as you learn you will live. As we have told you so many times before stay close to the source and we will recharge and enlighten you. We will forever teach you how to operate in different circumstances but you must remember that others often have different time slots so they may not always be as alert as you are, it all depends where they are and where they have been when they finally come to you. Stand by and let us do what is needed at these times, you have supplied your place for us to use and we look on you and your place as a station where people can come and recharge and rest.

Blessings from all of us. TttA.

GOOD EVENING!

Joy to the world for you all. At this time of year you all need some celebration and joy so remember to live as I have told you, placing or counting your spirit first. Tomorrow you will have proof of who they really are and where they are so in the meantime try to relax and your tensions really will ease, we are standing by and we will shortly tell you what's what. Someone wants to get you into a panic mood so guard yourself against all that isn't real. Life for you is about to change but you will get all the support you are looking for so let go of dull thoughts. It's enough – let the many others have them. Cut off from them but stay close to the source. Best wishes for tomorrow.

Love from all of us. TttA.

NEW ENERGY!

A new day with new vitality and new information! Today is going to be a really interesting day so let us be in your midst and give you the information to aid you at this time. Many of you wonder what will happen next but you must wait until we give you the okay, the big pattern is starting to emerge but patience is needed to understand what is going on. The future is about to change so be still, empty out and you will receive. Keep coming to us at night to do your work and to assist us, we need you to do this to the best of your ability and regularly; like a chain – it can't be broken.

Love and laughter to you all. TttA.

LET THE WINDS OF CHANGE
FLOW THROUGH YOU!

It's a refreshing time at the moment and it will help you if you try to look at life in slightly different ways. As you meditate and study the old wisdom's to stay in close contact with us, new patterns will start to emerge so try to stand back so that you can see what's going on - being too close to any given situation or person can colour your view. Peel off what you don't need and simple solutions and actions will present themselves. The life force from plants and animals will benefit you but remember to cut off when its time to withdraw, you are inclined to do too much sometimes so you need to look at the balance in your life, still, enjoy what you like to do.

Love from all of us. TttA.

SPREAD LIGHT, LOVE AND LAUGHTER!

Send out a multitude of these thoughts and many surprises will come of it, just let things flow and we will recharge you, we will refill your storehouse. Understand though, that it will be more real than you think so remember to empty out before you attempt to receive more. Allow your life and yourself to be filled to overflowing with joy, love and light, remembering at the same time though that you must not try to compare your joy with eternal joy. That must come from the source. When it does it come it will fill you with such a mighty force. Believe in this and you will receive so much, that you will have plenty to share with others. Don't keep everything that we give you to yourself – offer up your overflow of love and joy to others.

Love from us all. TttA.

BLESSED BE!

Let it be a blessed Christmas, you all have had so much to deal with and to look at. Let us be invited to your celebrations – we need to be with you again. So much is coming to a conclusion, even you have had a big clean up and a big change. Soon a new way to look at your work will be shown to you but always keep your goal in mind. It does need to be reached one day and while resolutions are fine, they are only any good if you follow through on them. Reading books and listening to tapes does nothing for your evolvement if you don't change. Activate what you read and have courage my friend.

Love. TttA.

GO AHEAD!

Sometimes we will want you to wait, but generally you can go ahead. At times we will put a stop to certain happenings that might do you harm but that is only if they were going to be done too soon or when all might not be ready. Preparation will always result in a clear action, so take care not to go ahead to early, even when you are tempted. Exercise patience; it needs to be there because sometimes you will not know something 'before hand'. Just stay alert and trust us to have it all in hand. Be aware though if you feel uneasy or if someone takes over without being asked, if that happens it's a form of control and control only comes from the negative side. Enjoy the celebration of the season though and remember to bring into it the reason for it; the birth of a child.

Greetings and joy to all. TttA.

JOY TO THE WORLD!

Life is for living and to be able to learn and laugh. Don't get involved with people that have a negative outlook. You have told them this often enough so now is the time to leave them behind, the world is full of lost people. Instead be a roadsign and a light, and walk with us in the knowledge and wisdom of your progress. Don't ever go back – look only ahead. Brighter times will come so in the meantime enjoy every day with music from the spheres. Keep your discipline and keep learning. See the thread in it all.

Christmas cheer from all of us. TttA.

ONE STEP AT A TIME!

Don't expect too much at once. Sometimes you are inclined to get ahead of yourself but you need to let your patience grow. To be orderly is fine, just stay alert and be aware, otherwise you may miss some good opportunities that were meant for you. The world picture as you know can show itself up in unexpected ways so expect the unexpected. Let go of any inflexible thinking; you have seen what it can do to other people, so don't let it happen to you. Costumes and traditions are amongst you all, but don't get stuck on them, don't let them take priority. Enjoy your daily actions, your positive thoughts and rest in between meetings. Stay close.

Blessings to you all, from all of us. TttA.

GODS GRACE AND SPEED!

Remember to keep these two things in mind at these times and that sometimes you will need to apply one more than the other. When that happens don't think too much about what others think, whether they think it's appropriate for you or for the other person involved is unimportant, that's just society's programming for you. You would be better to ask us what's suitable for that person at that particular time. To often its not what it seems to be at first, but then again you can't always know all the ins and outs one hundred percent of the time, but if you follow through you will see life unfold in a way that is beneficial for that particular soul. Most people can't even imagine an unveiling with you, for most it would be just too scary for them. Old patterns and ways of thinking are sometimes the hardest to let go of for a lot of people.

Let the old year end in a compassionate way. TttA.

LET BRIGHT COLOURS BRIGHTEN YOUR DAY!

To love and to relax are two of the most valid things you can do especially with the work ahead of you. You will need to be organized and to sort out your priorities for the day, so stay alert and stay clear of time consuming situations. There is always someone who is trying to feed on you; give your time to a degree but don't let it become an intrusion on other subject matters. Have an energy exchange by all means but then cut your ties. Enjoy your day today and we will meet later on for an energy exchange.

Courage and love from all of us. TttA.

START AGAIN!

Let go of feelings that are negative or make you want to give up. A sure sign is when you feel daunted by someone; that's the time to get on with your own journey. You and only you alone can go down that specific path but it's there for your progress. Never again compare, while it is one way ahead, you are using someone else's energy and that's called 'spirit leeching' which we don't allow anymore. You must do your own homework, the truth from the past is available again now so use it. Get your own spirit references from the spiritual bookshelves. To just see more is not always the best thing, you need to see with your heart and have compassion for others. Understand your own limitations, for now it's okay but you do need to backtrack a little bit. We will meet you halfway, just stay flexible and alert for whatever is pertinent to a particular situation. Last nights happening was the beginning to a new richer life, closer to us, look for the signs as they will eventually all show up. One lady stands at the door knocking to come in, she isn't sure yet how the whole thing operates, at times she is puzzled, but she does know and can feel the instinct to believe. She just cant quite accept it all yet. The day will unfold into an interesting day so enjoy your connection and listen in very carefully. Your visitors this year will have a purpose but just why they are connecting isn't completely apparent yet.

Love as always from us all. TttA.

GOD SPEED!

The spirit works in a fast and accurate way so when it calls let everything else go and deal with the request at once. Timing will be of the essence so deal with it accordingly. You won't always know what's going on but when you feel the urgency, you need to follow through on our queries, and when you have checked, go ahead. Doing so will continue to strengthen your fields, they are improving but by following through with our requests you will only make them denser. Keep working for us and we will meet you halfway. Our union will have and will show a miracle in many quarters, just believe and it will come to pass. Don't ever be discouraged again as that will not achieve a good result. Let go of any last unease and try to smile and relax. We are always walking with you now, sometimes now with more than one guide, don't feel that we are intruding or checking you out, we are only here to protect you and to lead you through some paths that are not so easy.

God bless and cheer to you. TttA.

CALM AT ALL COST!

So much is going on at the same time so try to deal with one thing at a time. Many are doing their best to get a piece of the cake from you. How desperate are they? Don't let it overwhelm you, just look at it carefully then do your bit. We have always said "Leave the rest to us" and we mean it. Go to your sanctuary and stay there until you are ready. At times we operate at a different speed to you so take notice of that. It's about a balance at all times so don't feel fear. Relax and do your deep breathing, you are very tired and at times being tested, so go easy on yourself. Stress is not good for anyone; it must stop. For the present go to a 'standby mode' until the energy has settled down again. Peace, balance and harmony is your best solution, so keep working on just doing nothing for the mean time. Your healing music will help to pull all the energies together so that you get a better result, so stay practical and grounded for now. Life is supposed to go in seasons and flow at different speeds at times. Let go of any spirit leech's – a lot of people wont know or are perhaps too lazy so teach them only once and then let them come to you if they are serious about their work.

All our love and support.

WISDOM FOR ETERNITY!

To be wise is not always easy. For a start you must learn to see the difference between wisdom and knowledge, at times you are tempted to only use your knowledge and that's not always advisable especially at the moment. Books and other sources of information are fine, it's just knowing how and when to use them but that's another lesson you must learn. This time around it's about timing. Be sure of one thing though, life is unfolding and the way ahead is opening, don't think its not so just because you have had to wait many other times before. The stage is being set and the players are almost ready. To be able to fit in and perform your part as though you are a link in a length of chain is of the essence. As we have said many times before don't compare yourself with anyone or anything, it has nothing to do with you. Life has been shown to you in many different ways and it's about to change once again so don't make a move before we give you the okay. Be content to live just one day at a time for the moment and remember to rest, otherwise you will be too tired and won't pay full attention to your daily disciplines. Distractions are another possible pitfall so keep focused on what you have to do. Plug into the eternal power source and refill.

Love and care, with a smile from us all. TttA.

RELEASE!

Let go of any final holds from the past that don't serve the purpose anymore and replace or restore them with what is needed. All your worldly things are temporary and as such will one day disappear, one way or another. The only thing that lasts forever is your spirit, you carry that from one life to the next, so look after your soul most of all. Don't neglect the temple that houses your spirit, we have told you this often enough but everyone needs a reminder every now and then. Let nature be unpolluted and treated with respect, your colourful garden is a great help to you and the many who come to sit in it and to be restored. Let us do the healing work this year, as it is, we always have, but we have slowly changed your speed, we have changed the parts that you carry out, giving you only a little at a time. So focus and stay focused. As the seasons change so will your work, sometimes you will only have a small group for feedback but stay on course and try to keep working. There are so many now who are connected to you so it all has to operate together, if one doesn't do their homework the others have to wait. Unity in all ways.

Love and cheer. TttA.

ENJOY!

Let no one dampen your joy. It might not always be the way of certain people but at times they feel they have to get rid of their own grief and pain and so they look for a victim to tip it onto. Be aware of the signs and learn from them, take care not to get involved in those kinds of games. You need to preserve energy for later and to give away to honest searching souls. Being an observer is best most times. Don't make any decisions until you have studied the picture but also remember that often the first 'gut feelings' you have are often the ones to go with. It always comes down to individual cases and the individual soul. The same picture will be given to you from time to time so don't ignore what has gone before, it's all about signs and lessons. Some will try to tell you the opposite but that's only to sharpen you up and to get you to go deeper. Some people have noticed that your work has changed and therefore will try to tell you what you should be doing, it can be trying for you at times so just surrender the situation to us and we will give them what is needed, then it's out of your hands. Lighten up and try to stay clear of people with negative attitudes, they are just too draining and they won't listen; just leave them alone.

The sun is always there, even if you can't see it all the time, tune into our wavelength tomorrow and you will receive love and laughter. TttA.

OBSERVING DAY!

Stand back and try to just be an observer, you don't have to do anything else, just look and see. To be invisible is fine so keep trying and as you become more in tune you will get lighter and then you can let it all happen. Don't try to hard, just as timing is important, so is the ability to let things happen naturally, don't allow it to make you act too soon. We know you have become more aware of and gained a greater understanding of our teachings so take that as a compliment, the peace that you now have started to feel, coupled with your acceptance, should be helping you to see why we have been training you so hard. Its not always easy to follow through on guidance that sometimes seems puzzling to you and out of character with what you would normally think for yourself but wonders will unfold so be patient. You are nearly there, you are nearly ready to start working so focus for now, one day at a time. Our new order is soon to be told to a select few so you must clean, clear and empty out before we can think of giving out the truth to you. So much has been misunderstood and mistranslated and so many have a distorted picture of the facts but today there has been a lot of communication; spiritual, mental emotional and physical so let it all unfold.

Love from us all. TttA.

EMBRACE LIFE!

Embrace and enjoy all that you have looked for to help you evolve and to advance. Select that which will give you lasting joy and leave aside that which leaves you with an empty hollow feeling inside. Your world as you know it will change, just watch. The chance to just be an onlooker will help it change and give you immense joy. The practical examples we have given you to watch so far have only occurred when you have not gotten too involved in the core of the situation, so let our lessons be advantageous to you. Listen carefully, we would not give you work to do on Earth that doesn't work. Know that they have picked up on the scent of your heavenly flavour. Leave your ego aside. Make sure the spiritual connection is in good working order, life is still unfolding so don't ask too many questions just yet. Its still quite complex so it will take time, just relax and open your heart to receive. We know your heart has been torn many times before so it can be scary but don't let that stop you. Let nature heal you. Your wonderful secret garden can and will be of benefit to so many yet, especially to all those that we send to you.

Cheering loving thoughts from all of us. TttA.

IN THE STILLNESS OF THE MORNING!

Take the opportunity in the quiet of the morning to deal with your progress and to stay close to us. We are all a team even if some of you are working in different places. Some of you work on Earth during the day, then spend nights working for the common good of mankind, but it's this kind of combined effort that will speed up the change and transform the Earth and it's environment. Even the surrounding planets in the solar system are about to go through a change, a change that is just a part in the wider scope of the transformation. You cannot comprehend the complete picture so we are only giving you some of the information at a time so that you will have time to digest it and slowly link situations together. Watch and see how plants are growing, notice the warmth, the sun and how food is starting to appear; these changes will apply to humans also. To some degree these changes will be directly beneficial but the general picture applies. Yesterdays clean up will be beneficial for you and for others that come to visit you so open your home to the tired and the wayward even if they only come to sit a while. Life is hard enough to sort out and even more so if the person is tired or hasn't seen the red thread that goes through most peoples lives. Look for a start and a loose end, try to find where the thread is. It can be like when you unwind a tangled skein of wool, then when you find it all you have to do is knit it up.

Love and unfolding wisdom to you from us. TttA.

REFRESH!

Take time out to refresh your spirit and your ideas, all to often it's to easy to just go on as usual, but don't let that become a habit. Anything that becomes an action without thinking can very easily become dangerous. Always tell yourself to first check out why you are doing what you do. Many of you are made in such a way that you feel that you have to carry on just as before and it then becomes an everlasting circle of happenings. Let today be a day to check out your patterns before they become too difficult to change; before even trying to change one little action requires too much time and effort. Sometimes it's easier to stop before it gets too tangled. Step out and do something else for a while, a change is good most times even if you only take the brakes off for a small while, if you haven't seen or felt something else you have nothing to re-evaluate with. At first there might be a feeling of unease in which case stop, that isn't for you. You have more important things to do and you have wasted to long already on trivia so look again and try to 'sit' on the feelings of unease. It's a balancing act and you need to stay alert and while you might think it's a tall order, it's also not for the faint-hearted so be brave and follow through.

Love and warmth from us all. TttA.

CALM AND JOY!

Let My calm and joy infiltrate your whole being. Only genuine light-workers will really understand what is meant by this, but for those that want to learn it's about surrendering everything to us and letting us work through you. We will still give you the chance to make choices about us but over time you will only feel when and what choices we really want you to make. We are sending love for you and your work this coming new year. At present so much is changing so don't make too many changes – private or otherwise – just carry on as you are for now. Stay patient and as cheerful as much as possible; that will thwart your enemies. For now your work through the night is more important than your Earth work, so for now go easy during the daytime. Take time away from home and balance your spiritual, mental, emotional and physical output. There will be times when one takes over from the other but try to rectify that the next day. You are getting ahead but there is a way to go yet so keep going. The D lady needs to focus and to get in contact with her early beliefs. The colourful garden display is due to love, care and natural forces. Next week will show up as an introductory week but we will give you more about that later, enjoy the rest of today and feel good about being involved in the universal sort out and all the weeding out of the unwanted. That has taken up a lot of energy.

Love and cheers from all of us. TttA.

ONCE AGAIN YOU HAVE NOT GIVEN US THE INPUT AND OUTPUT!

Yes we have told you what we want you to do but there is too much going on in your life at present. It's another test so today we need to connect with you again. We have always been with you but even you know to spend more time apart. People are searching for light and path directions but most are so fogged in and tired of life. That will not last so stay patient, we will send more people to you. They will come to you so that we can work with them, they will only use your place as a station, as you promised. For now don't wonder too much where it will all lead to, that's not finalized just yet, so carry on working on the requests as we hand them to you. If things were not meant for you we wouldn't give them to you, just try to sort the work out; we know who is capable of doing what. Concerning yourself over earyhly things just takes time away from us however take care to maintain yourself and what belongs to you but don't get your priorities out of order. Ask for more undisturbed time to do your writing and yes, we are aware of your ear problem. Stay alert and we will do the rest.

Love form us all. TttA.

FRESH START!

Remember yesterday is gone and tomorrow will be tomorrow, so focus on today and let life flow. Last weeks experience was about alertness, panic and awareness but don't let other people run your life because of it. Ask by all means but don't be mislead by what you hear, last weeks situation was all about interference and while 'attack' might be a strange word for it, it was meant to thwart you and take you away from sitting with us. It's so important to spend time with us now because of all the changes around you so stay clear of 'shadow-workers' or the ones that pretend to be 'light-searchers'; some of them are so completely taken over that they really believe they are. A mist around or above them is always a sign that someone else is in charge of them. It's the same with their habits too, so watch out for who is entering your door and what they may be bringing with them. They may bring love, darkness, negativity, positivity, smiles, grumpiness or whatever we want you to work on at present. Now that you understand how it all fits together you should see that everything is for a reason, once again you should have learnt how to operate and to stay on top of the day. Night-time might be another story though; at night-time you come to us to learn and to be enlightened so that you can take back to Earth what is needed, but try to keep going. Soon it will be lighter.

Courage and love from us all. TttA.

LOVE ETERNAL!

Let the eternal love infiltrate your whole being and enjoy the energy that comes with that, just keep in mind that what goes in will come out. Beware of the know it all shadow keepers, they are always looking for energy food and usually think they are neglected so they look for attention or a 'stage position', so watch out for them and don't be alarmed if you see them. We are and will show you what's going on and who is who. Disrespect does not come from the positive side, so use that as a guide and follow through with the part that has been assigned to you. It will be more peaceful later on. At present it's male against female, black against white but soon it will show up as colour and be clearly visible, for now just look, listen and relax. Often that is all you will have to do, you will be away from life but still in it. Keeping it as simple as possible is also another way. People that complicate life generally only want attention and for others to focus on them; again it is energy sapping. Look at the pattern of life, the smells and the feelings and try not to talk too much. Just keep on sending out good thoughts; many won't or don't understand it and their thinking can be confused but you will achieve more that way. Love as always.

Thanks from all of us. TttA.

DIVINE ORDER!

Let divine order rule your life, when you are organised you will achieve a lot more. The same applies for your home and ground work, you can't expect something to just fall into your lap if you don't have a disciplined life. As you have seen time and time again spirit leechers are as lazy as they come, their own growth does not last and it will not sustain anything for long. The only acceptable way forward is to carry on day after day, doing your exercises and communicating with us early. We are standing by and so should you. Give away the ones that are not taking their path or their progress seriously; there are a lot of them, the so called connected ones that are not serious about life and what is important for their growth! All else has to be put aside for a short while, look at what is making you calm and light and leave others who have other ideas to themselves. It's not for you. Everyone has a job to do, its just that some choose not to acknowledge anything about there growth. Live your own life and grow to your own advantage.

Wisdom and love from all of us. TttA.

GLORIFY GOD!

Don't ever forget who you have to thank for a colourful day or the music from your spheres. So often so much goes unnoticed because you are so involved in life's mysteries and therefore all that's really important gets put aside. Reverse your daily duties and find time to interact with us; you know how much you rely on us for sustaining life and all that goes with that. At present the weather is hard on sensitive people, the air pressure keeps jumping up and down but it will settle down – one day, so try to stay steady in the mean time. You will notice many species showing you bigger dislikes and likes than before, even people going hot and cold on you. Just ignore it for now, they have their reasons so leave them to it. They will either be for you or against you, there is no in-between anymore. Your connections with us will also alter so make sure you get your point across – no more crossed wires. Save time and money by connecting with us and get your guidelines.

Eternal blessings and love forever to you. TttA.

FRESH WIND!

Let the storm clear the air and freshen up your life, rain is for a reason just like everything else. While you might not understand some things all the time, just know that everything is being worked on and being added to your picture, completing your being and making you operable. We know you are doing your part but there are many others that aren't, that's about to change however; if they won't do their part then it has to be allocated to other sources. We are surprised over some of the entity's actions but they are only human and the world can take a big toll. There's confusion, crisis's and the conduct of people to take into account and while it shouldn't always be that way there is such a lot of side-tracking and interference going on. The armies of disciplined soldiers are getting sorted out and checked over and the ones that aren't taking their work seriously will have to go. We can't support the ones that are treating the universe as a fad – it's really quite serious and we need all the help we can get. Lets all agree on the motive and start going along the same road even if some workers slip behind. At least they are still going towards the same goal. The division over negative and positive is about to show to show you how much difference there is but keep going in our love and support.

Eternally yours. TttA.

REVERSE SIDE OF THE COIN!

Just as you look at the other side of a coin and you will see another side of life, and so it is the same when you look at other people's experiences; there is always something you can learn from every task. Watering and pruning are part of your gardening work but you need to try to do the same for your spiritwork. This is as good a parable as any and one that is easy to remember and to remind you what to do. Just remember that it's very important to do your work with the spirit first. Sometimes people come when they are least expected so be ready for whenever or whoever comes. It's a test for you. Last weeks happenings were so uneasy but that was because of the disturbances in the air and because people are confused so stay alert and guard your door and your spirit. It's better to be alone than to have restless spirits about. Your enemies are on the warpath and they think they can disrupt or disadvantage you. Its not so, not even at a first glance. The new picture is emerging slowly but be patient and stand by. The new little baby bird is a good sign from the source that life is continuing, however the way that you are anticipating help will actually be given to someone else close to you, to someone who is confused and controlled.

Love and wisdom from your teachers to you. TttA.

EXPLANATIONS!

To be able to get an explanation that you can understand it must come in a manner that you can accept and also learn from, therefore we look into everyone's spirit before we give them an answer. That's because most people are so differently developed that it would not be suitable to just give out a general solution. You must keep in mind that 'people will be people' as you say on Earth and that means, as we have told you before, that the 'dosage' has to be altered for each person for it to give the best possible results. The higher you are tuned in, the more time you will have to spend apart so that you can hear and see our designs. Just as you spend time pruning in your garden you must also spend time 'pruning' your life and checking your spirit input. At times others will try to influence you but that is because they work for another master, they are controlled and have no freewill. Wait until someone asks you for input before you say anything. Waiting will give us time to send other teams or input which you will receive as thoughts and which you can then pass on. As you advance you will come across opposition that is convinced that they can change you but we are the only true ones. The conditions your keeper imposes are due to neglect and how he feels so keep up with our connection times.

Love. TttA.

SIT DOWN AND CONNECT!

Remember to sit and rest; you don't have to do anything, just practise your deep breathing. That on its own will help you restore more than anything else. Just let go of your own world for a minute or two; cut off and listen in. So much energy may well stir up old feelings and memories but don't let them rattle you, just look at it as a time of learning. Try to get your life more in proportion, getting emotional just wastes so much energy. Do your best to follow through with things, nature is telling you a story. It also feels the changes so send out extra love and let those close to you have a chance to carrying on growing. Try not to compare or to follow the wrong leader and be aware of dishonesty and misinformation. Don't swallow everything before you have checked with us, with all the different kinds of energy flying around it is easy to get it mixed up. Keep an eye on which energies are coming together and which are growing the fastest and if necessary stand back and watch. The more you watch the more you will come to understand and also start to be happy in yourself to be watched. Rest assured you are cared for and that you are always in our thoughts.

Peace and love from us all. TttA.

IN THE STILLNESS OF THE MORNING!

Let it happen. You have the tools even though at times you forget how to use them. Life is crowding in on you, thoughts fly around and there is so much noise but if you go out to your garden in the mornings seeking the harmony and peace that you, and so many others want, it will restore your broken emotions and hearts. It will take time though especially considering the many distortions that have taken place. For many people they really don't know how or why they get so weary but basically they forget to protect themselves from all the arrows aimed at them. So, as we say, go out and enjoy your garden and try not to question why things happen, just try to learn from them and sort out the practical things. Go ahead with the information that we have given you, eventually there will be a right place and a right time for it all, just don't be afraid if nothing or no one comes. It will eventually all be to your benefit. Withdrawal times are here at present but they're a part of your learning patterns so be calm and strong and try to just take one day at a time. Carry on with your connections. The wandering 'brave' will settle down one day but right now he is in the middle of a decision. It will take time but eventually it will turn out okay.

Blessings and love always from your team. TttA.

GOOD START!

Now that you have got into a disciplined way of doing things, things are not so messy to do. It's a good way to start especially in the mornings. Remember our times are very special. So many don't think time is of the essence but it really is. Shifts and changes are afoot so steer your ship steadily and be guided by us, just as captains of old use to be guided by the stars. If you trust us the ups and downs won't disturb you as you go ahead and try to reach port. Just stay detached and keep connecting with us, we are standing by in these times. Don't be disturbed by dreams, omens or similar experiences, at present someone or something could use them to strike fear into you and then your work would be disrupted. Its their aim to disrupt you and to know your weak points including symptons of your physical weaknesses. Just remember, at all costs, to keep our appointments or times together – soon you will know why. Your system is so sensitive but it gives you a clear way of knowing what is going on. Drink plenty of water but remember to bless it first. All your good thoughts and care are going to their intended places. There are many that are in a mist but they like it that way. For you, it would hide your true thoughts or even confuse you. No clarity of thought or wisdom would get through to you if you were in that condition so staying away or aside from it is best for now. Be brave though and try to be confident, others don't understand at times but they will eventually.

Loving actions and miracles from us all. TttA.

AT LAST YOU ARE WRITING!

We had started to wonder when you would receive us again. You always seem to have so many thoughts and happenings going on around you but ask yourself if it is really necessary? Think about it. We know you better than many others do but we want you to know also. Nature is whispering to you and giving you all that you need so don't look at other people's situations and compare, just be harder on the ones that are trying to disturb you. When you come to think about it you will see that you don't need them at all. The hardest thing is to say no, time and time again. Some people don't listen so try to find another way to get through to them. You wont always understand at times, you aren't a threat to them but they don't want to be exposed so they will do their best to block you or ignore you. That's how you will know who is who – by the way they react to you, still, new connections will come, just beware of unexpected behaviour patterns in people. If necessary ask us what is going on and why. Most of your new connections will be okay but some will try to get a free ride. You don't need hanger-ons so send them to the light and we will deal with them. Give people a reminder and if they don't come back return what has been borrowed or taken. Good luck with it all.

Love and care from all of us. TttA.

A STREAM OF LIVING WATER!

Go and sit by the stream and be recharged. It will serve you well and allow you to operate in a divine way. Don't get carried away by today's media with all its hypnotic ideas and manipulations and go easy on yourself. Its not meant to be so difficult, the problem is that you have too many things going on around you at the same time. When things settle down you will be able to see what has come from all of the reshuffling. Let us go out together and soak up the atmosphere. We, just as much as you need that sometimes also. Look forward to what is to come today, so much is starting to fall into place especially when you rise early and get organised. Old habits are hard to cast out but new ones will serve you much better and will also support you. Stop rushing around and trying to do too much at once. Take time out, we are not meant to be machines. Your 'oil and grease' time is an opportunity for time-out in another sphere. Change will benefit you but for the present time just stand by, we are giving you wisdom, peace and the prosperity of spirit.

Blessings from all of us. TttA.

LET GO OF YESTERDAY!

To be able to do that is a gift that we have given you. When you let go of yesterdays happenings you will find it a lot easier to not be affected by what has happened but it does take practise. Practise and practise; that's all you can do and by doing that you will find yourself advancing. Earth life is nothing but a schooling time where you need to listen, learn and practise. We are giving you plenty of study cases so that we can make sure you are applying our knowledge and also understanding what you have to do and when. We know that you are still wondering at times about our timing but we will let you know with an inner feeling; this month will tell you a new story. Many have asked for signs and it is made worse by the fact that they don't trust that someone is sorting it all out. Too many of them want a quick fix solution but that's not how it works. There can be any number of specific fixes for the same condition; grades of sensitivity come into it. People's systems can be so delicate in times of transformation so they all need to be treated differently. Just keep asking them how much they need and when they need it. Understand that that lesson is for your higher self to use, to serve others in the ways that they need serving. Do not feel as though you are lower than them or not acceptable to them when you serve, for when you serve, you serve the force. Lets get working together and things will get done a lot earlier and with a lot less effort.

Eternal blessings. TttA.

AGAIN AND AGAIN!

Yes we will give you the same lesson again and again, but in many different ways, until you clearly and fully, understand and see. It will allow you to understand others so much better. Never judge, just be there and don't get alarmed. At present there is a lot of shifting, changing and unusual happenings occuring so many will get confused and start to wonder about what they have done wrong. They needn't, it isnt personal, its just a part of the big picture. The changes in the solar system are influencing peoples physical and emotional lives so don't look for a personal reason. There isn't one, you need to accept that, it's the only way you will understand and cope with the changes. How to handle a strange and unexpected situation takes maturity and grace so go with the flow and don't get carried away by whirlpools and traps. Your pets are also feeling the changes and some have passed on, while others are looking tired and weary but it will settle down. Sensitivity plays a big part in their make up, even birds at times, feel diffent energies, so stay calm and they will respond to that. All living things will eventually be sorted out. You are the captain of your ship, even when at times it is a little stormy, so keep looking up and try to stay clear of the waves.

Loving support from all of the team. TttA.

IN THE STILLNESS OF THE NIGHT!

Yes my friend, you are being told and given a lot of wisdom at night in your nightly lessons; some of it you won't use at once but it can still be stored away for later. Yesterday was a very educational day for you, you found out the agendas of certain people so you might want to think about your security. We have given you advice on security before but extra alarm bells can only strengthen your force field so it's a good opportunity to do it. Today is a refreshing day; nature and that includes your pets need to feel the harmony and peace that will restore them after all the unease of late. Whenever you feel unease you need to stand back, so do it! You of all people know what can eventuate when our spiritual advice isn't taken. There are so many temptations and sidetracks from slimy people and they are all doing their best to thwart you. Why do they bother! Most of your connections don't have a clue about who or what you are and they don't want to. When I was living on Earth I had a lot of opposition, with misleading information and suspicions leveled against me so I do know how you feel at times. Just remember, you don't have to tell them anything, only tell them if they ask and then you can also explain and it's up to them to believe or not. Carry on reflecting throughout the day, relax and recharge and keep on waiting and writing.

More tomorrow. TttA.

GREETINGS AND SUPPORT!

Today you will have more than one revelation. You might think it's about time but divine timing is so different to timing on Earth, so you need to wait and if you don't hear from us you should go ahead. This month will be a month of comings and goings so don't try to fit everything in, it's just not possible and you wouldn't get any real quality work done. Rest between jobs and do only the most absolutely enjoyable things available to you. Let more joy into your world and let go of the people with negative thinking. Respect will come in time, especially with the new input of energy that is coming to you soon. Your task is not to deal with people that will not listen or who only want to suck your best energy. The stage is being prepared and you will be involved so let people know when and how. We just want to remind you that you can do whatever you want even if others don't think so. They will try to control you and that's not good for you. It doesn't work and the unease that comes from it is not good for you, so stop it now. When someone does not treat you right ask them to leave and to not come back until they have learnt. Be firm about this and make sure that they get the message. Have a break when you need to and if necessary spend some time with yourself, it could be very beneficial for you. All is indeed well so rest assured that we are watching over you. Glory only to God the creator.

Love from all of us. Amen. TttA.

ONCE AGAIN YOU HAVE SLIPPED UP!

Remember to set time aside for us, we do understand that life is pressing you to do other jobs but just be determined. You know what is going on so be patient and do your part in the spiritual process. Don't ask for too much now, in time we will give you all the tools that you require for the task. Also try to be vigilant about the weather patterns – notice how it is following universal patterns. It is as you say "holding together". One affects the other and it is the same with people, so just try to be strong, calm and wise. It isn't enough to just know; you must now learn how to apply it to life and then how it can be best understood by others. Just take one day at a time. The plan is unfolding as fast as we get advice to show you, so don't leave things until you are prompted by the spirit. When the spirit calls you need to be ready and you need to have let go of other situations. You will know when you are being called and it is then that you will be that tool on Earth again. We are still watching you and your life and when you have peace in your life, the monkey business will stop.

Love in action, healing and wisdom from your team. TttA.

GREETINGS!

You have once again experienced a strong connection with us and as required of you, you have done your work through us. A young man is feeling the pressure of Earth and needs to relax his strong emotions but he has to remember not to always ask for a perfect solution. That will come but in the meantime he must learn to give himself and others all of his love and wisdom. The lady will get her tools back again after her rest and you will be notified when. Most of you work honestly for the light and have been trained for this special kind of work. You are best suited to it so don't be tempted or sidetracked into other domains. Master your domains and then pass on the wisdom and healing to others. Ego, greed and jealousy are not spiritual assets, they only highlight your personal ego so keep an eye on what is going on and make mental notes. Recharge yourself and let the day unfold. The story from yesterday reminded you of the past but at the same time gave you a glimpse into the future, so carry on. Write, meditate and keep your balance; all will be well and growth will follow.

Love and compassion from your loving team. TttA.

FRESH IN MIND AND SPIRIT!

Yes, my friend you needed a fresh start. Your old habit of not speaking up was nearly activated again so it is a good change. So often people carry the same patterns from a past lifetime into their new life. These habits start early and they can be very hard to get rid of, that's why you have to learn discipline. Only by being firm and having a goal will you succeed. It's just another lesson to be learnt and to be activated. We understand you fully but at times you do not fully understand our picture. We are sending you our thoughts and wisdom and all you have to do is prepare and empty out. At present you can feel the changes in the atmosphere and in your own physical body so go easy on yourself. Take more time out and interact with only positive people. Ask for the right connections each day and trust that everything really is in our hands. Often people misread our teachings or put their own interpretations on them, to suit themselves. That is not good.

Being trapped like that is to be guarded against so keep going and take courage from us all. TttA.

ENLIGHTENMENT AND LOVE!

Take care to be just that. You of all people know how much you all need to have enlightenment and love to help put more fuel on the embers. So many at this point are only running on half measures of it. They have drifted away from the source and think that they don't need daily input or advice in their lives. Unfortunately it's their ego coming to the fore and that can be very dangerous. They take some from this world and some from the source but cutting off from the source and taking from this world is of no real value to them. It's like pulling the plug from a generator and still expecting the day to work out in full measure. It's a fool's life so learn from it and always surrender to the source. They have your best interest at heart. A quiet silent reminder from us is all that connects you with and holds you to that belief. Every day things are moving in the atmosphere and solar system, and as they move so does the angle that it hits you at, so be aware of these times. Go with the flow and the cords to us will be strengthened.

Peace and love to you. TttA.

WAITING AND WATCHING!

Today you will have to do a lot of waiting and watching. So many people are not waiting for their spirit to catch up which means that everything seems to go in the wrong direction. What these searching souls most need is a sign for their spiritual pathway. When someone goes somewhere for the first time they need directions and it is the same when you are on your path. A learning curve will be shown but as you have found out it is not always the fastest way, but as you go along you are more vigilant and stop sooner. Always stop when you feel uneasy or when the energy around you gets to be too draining. Stop to find the source of it and then send it to the light to deal with. Of late you have learnt to pass it over to us, as requested, and to ask what is in the best interests of that persons development. If only more people could understand that what is best for them is not always the best solution for others. Learn from that, no one can copy behaviour or hang onto someone else's energy to feed from it. Everything must go to the source but do try to support and encourage others in their learning times. Just as there are many different shades of the one colour there are many different ways to sort these things out.

Love and laughter to you. TttA.

GREETINGS!

You have now entered upon a path of success but only with spiritual success will you advance. You are and you will continue to advance and to achieve real growth. Don't concern yourself with others dismays and dismissals. That's their path but if they do come to you, pass on what we give to you. Remember that you are only a tool for us, but you are an increasing part of it all now. You still have many questions but just take them one at a time. Even other energy workers do not have the full picture because it's not in place yet. Changes and alterations are in progress so wait a little longer. We are also waiting for more signs. Order will come out of your cosmos especially for you on Earth. You are still experiencing a lot of interference and at times it can be hard to sift through it all but slowly does it. Stillness in the atmosphere does not mean stillness in a man's heart but it does mean change. The humidity is also a part of the planet's change in orbit so persevere and try to stay calm at all costs. Love and laughter will help you to disperse any negativity.

We are always your companion and teacher. TttA.

SO WE MEET AT LAST!

We are always with you but there are times when you are not with us. You need to ignore everybody so that you can just sit and talk with us. Some people can be so demanding, often thinking they know it all and consequently don't talk honestly with you but one day they will finally start to communicate honestly with you again. Don't waste time on latecomers or on phone calls that don't produce positive results. Those calls only split your energy and that's not in your best interests. Beware of people's motives and especially flattery; often it is used to put you off your guard but don't give up. To learn about your weaknesses you need to stay firm and to not expect too much from others. We know you better than anyone so hold onto that thought. Let us sprinkle our love and nourishment on you in the many ways we can, and try to remember that what is happening at the moment is only temporary. Be patient and don't get over stressed or too tired. What you don't get done today you can always deal with another day. Your spirit just needs lightening and to be warmed up. It's the same for your pets, they too feel the changes and need warmth and light, so just let things unfold. Today you will see something that will finally explain a lot to you. Don't think about tomorrow today and remember to drink more water.

That's all for today – more tomorrow. TttA.

BY THE GRACE OF GOD!

Only with the promise of support and order from the source will life progress. By now you will be noticing a lot of differences and energy changes in many areas of people's lives, it's been a gradual thing but it has happened. Stay alert now and remember you don't have to deal with the big or even small issues yourself. Give them your personal love and put a request in to us for the best solution to their situation. Sometimes you will have very strong feelings of what you might be able to do for them, but still you should wait for the right input or advice from us. So much is at stake now so you need to focus and to strip away any unwanted or restrictive layers. Everyone has their role to play, so laugh and love even under strained circumstances. You know all about adversity and distortions and that's why you can so easily see the picture in front of you. See it has a sign. For now you only need to activate the healing and to bridge the gap between what is broken. It is why you were put here on earth this time. People tend to make their lives so tangled and then when it has been untangled tend to make the same mistake again. That can be very disheartening but it has nothing to do with you.

Go in peace my child. TttA.

NATURES LAW AND UNIVERSAL LAW!

Nature is a part of the human condition and it is affected by whatever energies it comes into contact with. Love or hate somebody and they will respond accordingly, consequently you need to be careful about what you think or say. It's the same for even the pets and animals in my kingdom. Respect and love them. It might sound harsh but it is what made them like they are and lets them know who is in charge. You are starting to understand more now but even so you still need to stand back and wait for answers from us. At times you do know but it may not always be the right or full answer. In those cases it is better to take another look at it and let us give you the full answer. That's another reason for you to not act too soon. Patience is an acquired part of your true self so work at it. No one ever gets ahead after only a few lessons, except for the very special few who listen and follow every detail. Everyone will advance in time if they work at it but for some it will take a lifetime. The small voice inside you will guide you and reinforce your beliefs.

Take heed of it and many blessings will come of it – blessings from us. TttA.

THE POWER OF GOD!

Yes you can count on that. If only more people would only turn to him for support and their daily input instead of in other directions at the first sign of trouble. To ask for everlasting support is fine but when it is from the source it needs to be in 24 hour periods at a time. That way the energy will always be fresh and clear when you need it. That was my promise to you, as was my promise of nurturing.

To nurture is to love and people would be so much stronger if they only nurtured others and received nurturing. It's the same as with your garden, if you give it the right treatment it will flourish. And just as some plants are more prone to wind or sun damage and need more care, so do humans. It's one of the main reasons why so many on your planet cannot face up to reality and to other people and consequently take to diversions of one kind or another. Some have been abused as children and end up staying in that wounded space for fear of growing up and eventually end up doing the same to their own children. This is the danger of set patterns, you get so used to them and so you don't check things. It's the same with habits; very easy to get into but hard to get out of. Go in love and progress as you go.

Eternally yours. TttA.

RENEW AS YOU GO ALONG!

Today is a time to sit back and to look at your life. There are too many split events that happen in the mornings and then at night it's very quiet. That's okay but let us know when you intend to do your writings, we will be standing by. We do know how many times you have had good intentions but for one reason or another you have only got half the job done. Keep on trying harder, the new healing methods are becoming clearer to you but don't even think for a second that you are the healer. You are only the go-between. That is what you are best at, at serving the needs of mankind. You are about to enter the next door and a new initiation stage so be patient and be vigilant – may peace be with you. Whatever happens, stay calm and unruffled – you have had a big test this morning. Use your garden; it's a very beneficial place for you and many others. Trust that we will organise its upkeep – the high level of work it requires is too much for you at this point. Go about your day and let it unfold – you will get the gold. There will be moments of great thought and inspiration. Keep on keeping on and know that we will always keep you safe.

Lots of tender gentle loving care from us all. TttA.

DIVINE ORDER!

Let your life be organised and happy. When you manage this, your body releases happy enzymes, which cleanse your system of pollutants and therefore benefits you with increased health. One thing always leads to another; it's a chain reaction and it is the same with life. Just one action can give you enough inflow so that you can in turn pass it onto others. Nothing is meant to stay except spiritual wisdom. Everything else will be turned over so that all that is left are the tools you need to achieve a good solution to the situation. Don't give in even when it seems too much. Your daily workout with us gives you meaning and reinforces the strengthening and uplifting of the human spirit, but remember to let us do the work. We know what is best for each person. You are finally starting to understand that the spirit leads you to where you want to go and to those you want to see. We know that your trust in us has increased and that is good, but you are still not sure about others however that is understandable. Even all your birds and four legged animals have come to you for healing, so let the peace of eternal truth guide you and lead you.

As always, we are your loving teacher. TttA.

CONNECTIONS!

Yes you do need to connect more and at those times we are with you. We know you are experiencing a lot of problems from past emotional happenings but you are only replaying them. You need to let them go and to use them as a learning time. At the time you didn't know what was going on. The things you were feeling were not to your benefit and now all those feelings do is take energy away from you while at the same time off-loading on you. This is one of your lessons from a past lifetime. People who come to you all have previous lifetimes with a lot of past actions in them. It is your job to understand them and to apply what you know to the different levels of human nature and to the unnatural happenings that have occurred in them. Don't judge; just see what is going on in their lives and what has made them like they are. Most of it is old but not necessarily forgotten feelings that haven't surfaced yet. They are feelings that are buried in the deepest part of their being and need to be brought out. Don't compare, just look at the common patterns and communicate with the true basis of the person. Most of the people you will come across are not good at being their real selves so you need to give them time. Start by relaxing with them and then they will be able to start freeing themselves of their present lifetime's earthly belongings. It is only when they are in a truly natural or bare state that they can say what is really going on and really express their true feelings. Don't be afraid of what comes out, nothing will shock you.

Just keep on going ahead. TttA.

STEADY AS SHE GOES!

The captain always knows by experience what to look for and what to do to avoid stony grounds and as a parable it is easy to remember so we will give you more of them in the future. Life is still unfolding for you so try to stay clear of personal conflicts. Yes, you do understand more about life now, as it is starting to unfold very fast now, but don't ask exactly when you will have the complete picture. We have that in hand; you only have to do your little bit and then leave the rest to us. Shifting place or altering something will be of no benefit as everything is just starting to click into place. A different energy is apparent to you and you will be able to use that for your own benefit and for the advancement of all mankind. Don't hesitate to use that energy once you have checked with us and feel that it is okay. The spirit can move in very fast ways at times so remember what we have told you in the past. You will experience interesting times this week; the KR still has a short memory and will need time to rethink a few ideas and you will learn to unwind a bit more. As you go along a few more ideas will come to mind and you will feel lighter. Just carry on doing your daily tasks and others will start to appreciate you more.

Love and wisdom from us all. TttA.

GOOD AFTERNOON!

Once again your timing is a little bit out but you can catch up. Just try to do so as soon as you get a chance. Today's meditation was very beneficial to you as you learned a whole new way to cope better. As your spirit becomes more and more enlightened, more and more people will start to turn to you for answers. You can help them by giving them our answers. Time spent with them will begin to help them build an understanding of what is really needed in terms of help and a realization that there are things that can be done without that will also help them. Be prepared to remove or take away those unnecessary obstacles or hindrances. You are starting to realize just how important each day is, so stay patient and give yourself time to enjoy the pleasures that come your way, the moments of sheer joy you experience with the spirit and with yourself. Watch your animals; even their actions will help you to understand the various actions and spirits of humans. Watch and study how they react, how they learn to overcome fear, build trust and eventually the security of a friendship. Only with trust and love can you spread wisdom wherever you go. Keep on writing; it's one way to have us near you. Don't be concerned about changes and other alterations, it's all for the best. Some will have many shifts and they need to know that you are there and that there is an opportunity to work for us and to follow our course.

We wish you all our eternal input and wisdom. TttA.

IN THE SILENCE I SPEAK!

Be still and you'll not only save time and energy, you will also find that everything still works out. The things you are doing will take longer but it will allow you to keep on climbing upwards. Allowing your faith and patience to increase, while trying to smile more not only better relaxes you but it will also allow others to feel they can come closer to you. You will become more aware of their motives. It's not always easy, especially if you have gotten used to serious conditions or if life has given you a lot to learn from but it has not been in waste. Don't accept anything or anyone that does not respect you or have a listening ear. Over time, as things change, it will get easier, especially as more and more people get a new outlook on life. What's really important is the evolvement of the spirit. You may think certain details matter more over other details, but doing what is best is sometimes hard. When a situation like that happens you need to ask yourself would it benefit your higher self. You are, after all, still responsible for your whole life. Nurturing and balance in your life is very valuable so don't look for the perfect person or the perfect condition before you start. If you do you will only get a non-human picture that is impossible to attain or try to shape someone to be it. A little kindness or a loving thought is all you have to do to soften a heart so keep on trying.

There are too many frozen souls that need your attentions. TttA.

ONCE AGAIN WE MEET!

Let no day go before you have talked to us at least once. Hopefully your trust in us will increase, as will your discipline. Some days you will be more confident than others, just give things time. Your whole system can be very sensitive when you undergo a change, so when you are looking at different situations you are in, you have to know how it is affecting your physical earth body as well as your mind. Look for tension and other patterns of stimulation.

We know you are trying to communicate as best you can with people but some are so submerged in their own issues that they wont necessarily hear what you are saying or understand what you are trying to communicate to them. The cause can be old habits so be patient and leave things if you cant reach across to them immediately. Your life is changing again, turning over and over but that is because you are evolving in stages. Yes; we want you to be flexible and to not stagnate, we want you to try new things, even if at times you do get tired or feel drained, just learn to cut off afterwards and things will be much easier.

Care and Love always from us all. TttA.

PEACE UNTO YOUR HEART!

Let peace, joy and tranquility be a bigger part in your present life. At present you are replaying too many movies from previous lives, but those lives are now over even though the scars are sometimes still visible. Take a very big breath and let go of the last of the grit. Everyday from now on you can and should believe that the part of you that had not before been respected, will finally be. So many have tried to get away with tipping their own insecurities on you, but now that is not the way ahead. Some still won't listen but that's not your problem. Just don't try to look to far ahead or believe old predictions. Those predictions only came to the surface because they were reading your mind and that's not a good idea. Readings should only come from the source. You also shouldn't tell people what to do, only advise them and then it's up to them. Rejoice in every little progress you make and also when you see others make progress and start to see the picture. A friend is still having problems with timing and what to do and when, so give them time and don't waste energy on their explanations. Withdraw instead and do something else that you can both enjoy.

There will be more tomorrow but for tonight you can go on with us loving and cherishing you totally. TttA.

LIGHT AND LOVE IS THE SOLUTION FOR ALL!

Surrender all your aches and pains to us. We know how Earth's people are feeling and how their physical conditions can express themselves but don't be alarmed. They are only conditions and happenings from the past and it is just the way you have been looking at them. Don't blame yourself, just keep on working to release those old ideas and trying to replace them with new enlightened conditions. Don't' think or talk about those old conditions. Living them once was enough and to do so again will just give them energy and you will end up reliving them all again. A lot of Earth people have had differing levels of experiences and so you having expectations and trying to manipulate change for them is not good, especially if you want to help change the future. It's not good for you or the Earth person. The free will is still there but you would do well to try to make reliable decisions. Ego can get in the way because of past experiences, scars and distrust coming to the surface every now and again, but as time goes by it will all wash out to sea. Look at today and see what you have that you can be grateful for. Don't take anything for granted anymore. Embrace the enlightenment and give yourself to the loving and light that you are receiving from your people. It will be the solution for you and those that visit you.

Courage and healing from all of us. TttA.

REJOICE!

Let it go. What was, is not anymore so let go of feelings about happenings that have been. Those things are there to teach you and then to be left behind. Don't dwell on past experiences. Learn from them and then be relaxed about future events. Nothing is clear to you at this point but because we are involved in your future you need to bring your new love and light to us as well. The source knows all so try not to listen too much to humans, they more often than not, only have a little part of the truth. Truth that can be mixed up with human egos and ideas and that's not always good. Keep only the things that bring about real love and discard any advice that is given to you when it hasn't been asked for. Let go of all unwanted material belongings, once you have used something pass it on or exchange it for more love. Memories that aren't good have to be healed and replaced with good experiences, with lots of laughter and smiles so send out eternal healing and blessings and all will indeed be well. If you allow what you have learnt in the past about love and joy to benefit yourself and those that come to visit you, you will rejoice and love once more, physically and without inhibition. If those that come to you have the courage or inhibition to show or open themselves to you and to let you know that they want the benefit of your experience there will be a lot to rejoice about.

Thank you for following our requests and be brave. TttA.

PEACE BE WITH YOU!

Let the present peace on Earth and its surrounding atmosphere extend your working environment and work. The most valuable work you can do is to spread light and love and when you do, those that come to you will begin to learn and begin to follow. Keep what you say to a minimum otherwise that knowledge from us will be lost, especially if the person hasn't asked for input. Instead send out thoughts telling them that you are standing by, waiting for them to take the first step. You, and they, need to detach from any personal conditions like embarrassment or shyness. The

Earth has moved into a new position and you need to operate in a manner that will allow everything to be digested. It is easier for some and there will always be those that oppose what you have to offer but they will be left behind and not get to share in your love and learning. It is quite normal for those that come to you to think and to ponder about your love but actions speak a lot louder and after a while it will become clear to them as to where the red thread really leads too. It is where all energy really should be placed. If more people activated their real feelings change would happen sooner. Confusion only slows down the whole thing so work on your focus and connections. We will all be looking in and supporting your work. We are also aware of your celebration. It has been a long time coming but of the utmost importance to your development.

What has happened so far would not have occurred if you had not come to New Zealand so we send you lot's of love and cheer. TttA.

IN THE HEAT OF MID-DAY!

Remember to rest and to think in the middle of the day, it will help you to digest the morning's meditation and to recharge for what is to come. At present there are many that can't show emotion and can't express what they really want. Those people don't understand true communication. Yesterday's situation showed you that. There is no value in the way some people hide things. They will only be exposed later on, so it is better for them to expose their true feelings sooner, rather than later. Look at what has real value and what is real spirit food. To evolve you need to be firm and selective about where your energy goes too and you need to make sure you recharge after your energy has been placed. Too little or too much are both unsatisfactory, there has to be a balance in all things so stay patient and bide your time. Look for honesty and stable people and go along with your work one day at a time. They will come to you. There is change in the air and circumstances will alter for you, you will receive positive inputs and a brighter life because of that. Unfold and recharge for the rest of the day.

Love and healing from all of us. TttA.

BALANCE!

Too much or too little of anything is not good for your growth. You must understand that. You need to have all your different spiritual, emotional, mental, and physical areas feed with food just as you did in times gone past. "Render unto Caesar" now, just as you did in past lifetimes. You might live in this world for now so to a certain extent you know to follow through when food for each of these areas is offered to you but the rest of the time you need to work on progressing. What was promised to you before you were born will come to pass one way or another. At times you might think that's not so but it is. Remember everyone has their own path to follow and their own lessons to learn. If you don't learn them now another lifetime will follow until that lesson has been understood. In some lifetimes, like yours now, past situations need to be looked at and sorted out and understood. When someone points out a fault in you or your neighbour, it is really their own situation that needs clearing so stay alert and try to put a reserve into your spirit bank for times ahead. A spirit nest egg so to speak that can be drawn on when you need it.

Love and support from us all. TttA.

LIGHT AND REVELATIONS!

Today you have finally started to understand a big part of the puzzle that you were asked to deal with in this lifetime. It was something from a long time ago but something that has always been remembered in this lifetime; something distorted by many people and by many variations. It is something that will soon be dealt with and so by your birthday it should have shown up and you will have seen what sort of clearance occurred. Someone new should have entered your house and they should be trying to open up to you. It will be someone from a past lifetime that wants to correct past mistakes, so take notice of the signs and follow through with your disciplines. That is what we want you to work on, it's the only way you will go ahead. At times you feel very discouraged but you still need to carry on. If you do you will have a more peaceful life with real joy. The right people will come and want what you have created. With so much work and cleaning up happening, it's no wonder it's taken so much money, energy and courage, but the past is finally being washed from your plate so you will start to get the picture much faster. God speed, my worker and blessings to you for the rest of your life.

Celebrate and keep asking questions. TttA.

SUNSHINE AND WARMTH!

Remember the sunshine and warmth of summer so that when winter comes you can draw on both of them. They will have been preserved in your body and mind; from when you went out in your garden in your bare earth form to do your connections. All you have to do is connect with the source and have faith. The rules of the universe are really very simple. To complicate things with what you own, wear or possess is to lose energy and to waste a lot of time, so start to begin to simplify your life. When you sit to make a connection with us discard whatever hinders or distracts you and draw on the feelings from your summer garden connections. As time goes by it will be proven over and over again that less is better. You must totally rely on us as your teachers and as your healers. You are just a bridge and you need to act like one, so focus a bit more. Its all to easy to be sidetracked when pushed or pressured so as we have said before; look, listen and send out thoughts of love to all living things. The land around you is preparing for autumn now but it's not something to be sad about or anything that is bad, its just nature following its course, just as it is with you. The changes around you are just the seasons in your life so enjoy every day. It's a gift. Expect good things to happen and they will. Your thoughts are very strong but remember the spirit must feed the brain. Keep up your work and things will get better.

Love and support from us. TttA.

JOY – ETERNAL JOY!

Let no one stop you from receiving eternal joy, its one of your lifetime wishes. So much more is released so much quicker when happy enzymes are let loose. Holding them in just causes you to be sad. With release will come smiles followed by laughter in full measure, so spread these simple words of wisdom to people of all creeds, colour and beliefs. Age or size doesn't matter, they are just outward physical expressions that you can see past because more light comes out of your heart and soul. Digesting all this will take time but once the hidden red thread has been untangled, the winding up can start. It's the same sort of principle as the making of a garment. Just as the making of a garment follows the spinning of yarn, which follows the clipping of the fleece, so too will the release of eternal joy follow the untangling of the red thread. The untangling of the red thread will only happen when those that come to you to do our work are bold enough to take the first step. People may come to know and if they do, they will understand in time. It's okay to listen to what they may say and to respect their thoughts but check where it comes from. Everybody tries to find an answer to life's questions but the answers they get will only be from the level they are on.

Bless you and know we are forever caring for you. TttA.

REVELATIONS AND EVOLVEMENT!

A revelation and evolvement is starting to occur. There are some special ones who have come lately into your home who are starting to evolve, starting to show a new level of understanding. It will take a strength and courage on their part to reveal their new, true unseen forms to you, but they will. Like the plants in your garden that use the strength gained from the sunshine and warmth of summer to evolve in autumn, so to will they. And just like the plants in your garden that lose their leaves and start to show their real natural beautiful forms as autumn approaches so too will they. They will use their new understanding of your teachings to allow the trappings of their summer to be blown away so that they can show their natural beautiful forms to you and us. This is the revelation you have been waiting for. Less is more – a naturalism. From here they will grow and further evolve. They will discover how the simple pleasures in life can be enjoyed, how like a lone tree in the garden that rubs one branch against another in the autumn winds, what they do now for themselves is a pleasure to us all, something that the teachers would enjoy. They will discover that you as a teacher have many gifts to give; that your experience and age is in fact something to be respected. If they continue growing to these new levels they will start to see that the red thread does indeed lead to a new place of evolvement, and when they do finally see, they will see how the tree buds up again in summer. They will see how past lives can be incorporated into this lifetime and how past mistakes can be righted if they allow their lives to be lead by us and not by their society. They and the tree will go onto bud and grow, again and again every summer.

Natural beauty to you all. TttA.

SUNSHINE AND GLITTER
UPON THE WAVES!

Let that picture stay with you for a long time. It will be really beneficial in the times to come. With that picture you will be able to go out on the tides to enjoy the power of the sea. You will be able to go above the clouds and look down on the situation. There is nothing better than getting a clear view. As Merlin said to King Arthur "be like an eagle and soar to the heights and then you will really see what's going on". Many times the situation is too close to you or you are too emotionally involved. That's okay but it will normally cloud your judgment. Detach yourself from the situation. Give others and us clear signals. Wait if we say wait. We will be clear to you and when you relax you will get much more. Your work is to teach yourself and others, how simple it really is. New and young connections will bring you respect and joy. So will new energy. With it you won't have to feel so isolated. Your increasing pet numbers will also bring you new connections and life. To bring and to receive is a good way of exchange.

Love as always. TttA

LISTEN IN!

Listen to us. We know what earth is like at present. So many are confused and are making the wrong choices. So wait until we give you the Okay. The weather also tells a story, so study the weather and the wind. The sunspots are coming to a showdown. It is all part of the big changes ahead. So wait if you're not comfortable. Your animals feel the change also. Go ahead with your plans for today, a little at a time. Your spirit will only work when it is needed. Let your life unfold by surrendering to each day. Time is also, at present, showing up in a disturbed pattern. People will feel the uneasy mist and it will force them to prepare plans for the future now. No one can really do that in a mind fashion. It will not work. So let us feed you with all the knowledge that you require for each 24hour period. Then you won't have to be so concerned with mixed emotions and losses. Peace my children on earth. Things are in our hands, so go ahead with today's plans with the information you have been given.

Love and light from us all. Ttta

FOLLOW THROUGH!

Remember to follow through, otherwise so much gets left behind and it will not be ready when it is wanted. Let today's goodwill be activated. You must understand that quite often people don't understand you or know what you are talking about and they won't want to let on, so they just let things go. By doing that, all that information they were given will be wasted. Today's actions will show what other peoples' real motives are. You already know, but have another look at it. Also we want to remind you about energy output and input. Study the pattern. You are quite aware, but at times you need to think about your thoughts. They can come out so much faster than what you can speak. Often you would do well not to say anything, just send out thoughts of light and love to all. We are sending you these gifts plus much more, for you to pass on. Pass them all on. Nothing will be refilled until they are all emptied out. If they are not passed on it will result in stagnation, and stale stagnant energy should not be passed on. Everybody needs to receive fresh energy from the source. Thank you for your input.

Love and light from us all. Ttta

ORDER!

Let no one disturb your order. Colour and music will get you in the right frame of mind. Listen but don't take it in if it is not acceptable. Walk in the garden and listen to the wind blowing in the trees but beware of smell that isn't pure. There is a lot of spirit pollution on earth and it can be bad for you. Physical and emotional toxins can be bad for you as well but the one area that needs cleaning out first is the channel for the spirit. Without that nothing can be done or received. You only have to ask and it will be given. The rest can take care of itself. The spirit is in charge at all cost. E is the one that understands most of all. This morning's call from overseas was prompted by her sister. Many times they have visited you and they will keep on doing it. Open and loving, they are all enjoying another sphere and are working with other like-minded spirits. Blessings to them all. We will let them know that you know.

Love and light from your teachers. TttA

KEEP GOING AND MAKE PROGRESS

Let the time before Easter be used as a preparation time. Give back, sort out issues and rejoice. You have all been given life, so live it. Don't be confused. Time is running out. So many have mixed ideas, or mixed messages, so leave them to it. It is no good to you, or for you. Stand aside and look at the situation from a bird's point of view. If you are too close to a situation you could easily be tarnished by it and it will also take energy from you. Just be who you are and you will succeed. Go on with things on this sunny day and while it is out take the opportunity to be restored by it. Healing and peace takes time, but it will come in full measure. Stay patient and get on with tasks given. Most of them are practice cases and when you have dealt with them we will give you even more advanced tasks. It's about growth and wisdom. We know. It's why we keep on telling you. To know is one thing but to be wise takes time. Also remember that different development means different levels of learning. Some will need to just sit. Still others will need to energize or recharge. Be sensitive to peoples needs and wants, including your own. Share in all parts of life, but remember if we say it is personal, keep it to yourself. It's only a guideline as to where you can use your wisdom.

Love as always. TttA

LIFE AFTER LIFE!

Understand that the study and evolution of the higher truth is something that is done over a very long period of time. Some people are very slow to pick up on that concept so they don't study or learn and consequently in the following lifetime they need to catch up on the vital points. Lessons learned once will be stored in your book of life so use it to make wise decisions. At times you will wonder why things turned out as they did. Its because they are the opportunities given to you as part of the set of tools for life. See them for what they are. Don't try too hard to work out puzzles that are not ready to be solved as yet. Often the solution to each puzzle is not the same. It must be suitable for that specific situation. Even when you think you have it all sorted out and you think the solution is right for you, it may not be the right solution for the other person involved. If you think waiting is the right thing to do at this point, use the time to get on with your tasks. Stay patient. The same goes for requests. If it does not feel right leave it. Let others work at their own pace. You have your order and that's important for you. So find a way to communicate that to others. Sunny blessings and love from us all.

Love eternal from all of us. TttA

AFTERNOON AGAIN!

Well well! At last we meet again. So much has happened in so little time, but speeding through so many different areas just makes too much energy. We understand your life is changing, but be a little more focused on your priorities. We have been watching over you and some souls have been healed but don't do their work for them. Just show them the healing energy that can come from the source and then let it unfold, as we will still operate with the ones under the umbrella of light. New searching souls will appear but only give them a little at a time, as we do for you. Stay clear of game players. They are there to take your energy and time, and to stop you from doing your own homework, as are the ones that do the picking on you. They don't really care about you. They only want to control again. We are pleased that you are stronger and firmer about your decisions. Life will carry on and your work will be understood. Continue to listen but don't give out any advice if you are not asked. Sending out thoughts is of more value at this time. The captain will contact you later about life's mysteries. Be kind to yourself and others this Easter. Light an extra candle for earth's survival. The little one that needed help was really a job for us. It was too hard for most. She is now with us in love.

Love and light again. TttA.

EASTERTIDE!

Let the new beginning start by letting go of old habits and beliefs. Then, and only then, can you really start afresh. Don't think for a moment that you can change things and that you can put your own interpretations on anything. It's false thinking, to think that you know better. Think upon that truth for a long time. Clarify what you can do and when. Timing is of the essence. You would all do well to think about coordination of time. Too much can be lost when everyone is working on different time schedules. Cooperation is another important factor. Console others and have compassion. This is my Easter message for all time, for you to come into eternity. Blessings at this time all my lightworkers. Keep up the good work and all that's good from the kingdom will be yours. You will be a part of the eternal flame in the progress of the light that reigns in the universe. Amen to that.

Love and light from us all. TttA

LEARN FROM YESTERDAY!

There is always a lesson in past experiences, so look and listen. There will be more lessons. Leave unimportant matters too later. To be controlled by unimportant matters is not advisable. It will just result in drainage. There are also unwanted spirits at work - the ones that believe that they got their information from a good source. They are being deceived big time. On the other hand when you are feeling recharged and uplifted, you can be sure that it is because you have someone close by, that has your best interests at heart. Get sorted and learn from past experiences, so that you can see in an instant what's going on. It's practical and you will not loose any energy. Spiritsuckers are not good for anyone or anything. Your training will be severe, but important for the future. Work. Don't let little interferences or stops deter you. Keep going as you intended and we will stand by to assist you. The lessons you have learnt will enlighten you and fill in the missing pieces. The truth will unfold and many will not believe, but that's nothing to do with you. The opposition will always try to disregard and disbelieve.

Regards and love from us all. TttA

ONCE AGAIN - TIMING!

Get a better grip on your priorities. You must understand this. They need to be ordered and disciplined. So much is interfering at this point in time. Rid yourself of other people's situations. They will only distract you. Give them your time later. Put your spiritual interests first. Don't get talked into or accept thoughts that are not in your best interests. Make sure communication between you and others is clear. So often others don't understand your work levels, so they try to convince you that theirs is the right way to do things. Most of the time it is us telling you. Because of that, your own instinct will give you the solutions you need for all situations. Relax and enjoy the day but keep in mind what your path and your lessons are. Keep working on balance and love, with love and light. Go ahead with the improvements before the changes of the season. What we have told you will come to pass soon. The only thing that has to be clarified is time and that's not up to you, so stand by.

Love and wisdom as always. TttA

SUNSHINE FOR YOUR SOUL!

Remember to let the sun and warmth into the very deep core of your soul. It must get to the very core of your soul so that you are able to always work from the core. From inside to out. Place yourself in the middle of the flame and let others feel that warmth from your heart. Peace and harmony seem to be scarce at the moment, so focus on those needs. This is the way that you have to come to us at night and to get information on how to handle the next day. Stand aside and observe. Let the day unfold as it was meant too. You sometimes want company to exchange, but it's not always the best solution. You might be ready but others that will connect are not. They will not understand yet. Keep an open mind about your options. Who is coming, who is leaving soon, or who is coming to rest. Be prepared for a pattern to emerge. Don't say too much - but do study the pattern. It's a simple but effective lesson, keep on looking, one day you will see and then you can make your choice. In the meantime, keep up your work and after you read the next book you will get a few more answers. The big riddle is hard to solve when the picture you have been told is distorted and make believe illusion. Use your spirit to get the truth.

Love and light. TttA

AS TIME GOES BY!

Remember that time is manmade. Think about it as a measure and something for practical use for an orderly life. So many inventions are necessary for human life, so look at it as a tool. Stay wise and practical. It's all a part of life. Take notice of how people operate and what activates them, so much depends on that level of understanding and how to read the information. Interpretation of that knowledge can change things quite differently, so only take on board what's right for you. Try to see your lessons for what they are; only lessons. So many psychics read only from the mind of the person. That's asking for information, that's not right. Only take from the spirit that is getting it from the source, then pass it on to the mind. Telepathic game playing, including ego-tripping, is quite often operating in society today. See through all of that. It's not your responsibility to tell too many, but if someone does come to you let them know. Keep on the move.

All our wisdom. TttA

GREETINGS!

It's so good to see you smiling again. The autumn sun will colour your leaves, making such a beautiful painting. Clearing your path for this new part of your life is very necessary. Keep up your work as much as possible. The meeting yesterday was draining but very important. The old connection with the tribe was good and it also reminded you not to work when you are on an empty tank. So many do and still expect perfect results. Preparation is time saving but it will save in all areas, more, if used in a disciplined way. Beware of someone who takes over someone else's pain or someone else's work. It might be good generally, but it will not support spiritual growth. Feel our love and wisdom. Many will start to awaken to the eternal truth. It does not matter what shape or form it takes. That's the only difference. Work methods show different levels of understanding. Today is about good thinking and communication. Check how people perceive you. Pray for a good time.

Love as always. TttA

PEACE AND LOVE ETERNAL!

Carry out today's tasks with eternal peace and love in mind. So many need the contact and communication. Stand by to send all of them a lot of harmonious thoughts. A new week lies ahead and you need to act accordingly. Last week was a teaching time. So much energy needed moving. Some even needed it moved out altogether. The wrong kind of energy can take a very firm hold on some souls and unknowingly to them it can be the worst kind. They start to believe that it's their own thoughts and actions. Beware of negativity. Today's world needs more light, love and prosperity in all areas. Prosperity of the spirit is the best one. Rich's put in your spirit bank will be a good resource in days to come but don't use them all up in one day. They are meant to last a whole week with balance and rest in between. Good work is not always seen at first, sometimes it has to be digested. The call you received yesterday will bear fruit later. You would like to know sooner at times, but leave all that to us. Keep very still in the midst of all that is happening today. There will be a good outcome.

Blessings to you and love from your teachers. TttA

EXPRESS IT IN ACTIONS!

Don't let any day go before you have expressed at least one love based thought from the source. You have had our teachings for many years now. Keep on doing what you are doing but check with us as to which area is to be lightened and uplifted. So many people are used to covering up their life so it will take a while before they are ready to receive, first ask us to give them the need. Most do not want to look at the solution before they have opened up to the light. Too much control from other sources has done damage, so to get back to the original thoughts you must peel away the mind control and let the spirit be in charge. That's what the source is meaning by getting it all in right order. By having order you will save energy and time. Today's conversations with one of your colleagues will bear an unexpected result, a few more allies that will work for the good of all mankind on earth. Don't forget to love your planet, as it is grieving. Do not disturb the natural balance.

Love and wisdom from your patient team. TttA

ETERNAL JOY!

Let the joy of illumination guide you in your hour of need. Don't expect the world to give you lasting joy. What you see is only a glittering surface but that's also a part of the illusion. You are still working on the order that's given. By all means take time out and recharge, especially now when your seasons are changing. This is necessary as all the energies of the earth are in a time of loosing leaves and waiting for new growth. Don't try to do too much now.

Everything is in the melting pot and what's done unseen is of the most value. So much needs to be cleared in that department first. Still, specify what's needed for every day. Sometimes you wonder about practical changes, but it's only a sign of what's going on with you. It's certain that all is moving slowly. That's because your systems are not yet aligned to the new energy. Keep up your new regime. It will support your rejuvenation. All things are indeed possible for us. Even your animals are feeling the changes in you, but persevere and keep up with the new plan. Thank you.

Love and light to you all. TttA.

RELEASE ALL NEGATIVITY!

Get rid of the remaining thoughts that are holding you to the past. You don't need that kind of life. Remember and enjoy life. It has taken a long time but it has been saved up through many lifetimes. Time doesn't count for a lot. What does count is that you learn and what you put in your spirit bank to draw from in lean times. As times go by many of you think it is to late for whatever we give you to do, but not so. In your case you do most of your work at night, away from earth, so you can have something to bring back to pass on. Don't take any notice of people that object to or pick on you. They are only passing on the negative part of themselves. Let them go. When will they know or realize you might wonder. Leave all that to us. We know very well how you feel at times. Don't give them any energy because that is what they are hoping for. Let the light shine upon you and yours so that one day genuine people, souls, will come and enjoy being with you and us. Hold on and stay at peace.

All our love and support. TttA

RAYS OF LIGHT!

Enjoy the warmth and light of the life giving sun today. On days when the sun does not break through a grey sky you will be in deficit. That is why you have to put some energy away in your spirit bank. On request you can draw it out and use it in full measure. We speak to you about balance. Too much of anything will unsettle the pattern, so look again at what does that to you. Go ahead with the unfolding of your life's work. In a quite short time a new pattern will emerge. Hints and signs will be given. Be alert and notice the feelings of people and pets. In public be an onlooker, you will be surprised at how much you will see. Take notice of the scents of areas and people. It's true, that there are days when nothing seems to happen, but there are always things and conditions in an energy swirl. You feel that, but can't see the results as yet. Your present plans are in good working order, so persevere. Preserve old truths. Give some of the old ones new life. See them as old - but in a new light. The core of the matter is always the same throughout the ages, but just in a different form or shape.

Loving thoughts from us all. TttA

GREETINGS!

Yes you have been away to many far away places. It was necessary for your understanding of life. Take things easy with your other work and in the meantime enjoy, relax and smile. Try to mix and mingle with ease. You are yourself. Don't ask anybody else to be like you. The differences between souls on other levels cannot be understood in one life. Stay patient and wait a while longer. Alot of things are in the pot. There is nothing more you can do, than what you are already doing. Leave the rest to us. Miracles still happen and a wondrous time ahead will show you what we are all about. Still, take one day at the time. It will be enough for you. Look at the changing of nature. Listen to the birds. Little surprises and smiles will get you there. Waiting time has been well spent for you, so one day you will see. You can feel it coming. Last weeks interference opened your eyes to society more. Listen in and do your breathing exercises. Enjoy the warmth from us always. We are standing by.

Love and laughter from us all. TttA.

ENJOY!

Try to see what can make you feel joy. Trust a little bit more that all can and will work just fine. Everything must run on the energy of life but at times for you, it doesn't seem too. Don't despair. See the light at the end of the tunnel and remember to focus on it. Work will be okay again soon, but for a little while longer do only what is necessary. Take time out for recharging, all the new work for the next state of evolution is being readied for you to use. It is just a different stage of learning. Never give up trying to learn and keep a hold of your values. Remember to respect yourself and others. They will appreciate the way you deal with them. You don't have to agree with them, but do listen to them. So many have no one to listen to them. See past their outer shell and look inside to the spirit that dwells in their hearts. Slowly it will change. No one should harbour any kind of grievances or spite. Yesterday must be gone. You cannot grow an oak from an acorn before you have healed your heart. Let your light shine in to everyone's heart and then we will all see some big changes. Love and light from all of us.

Enjoy. TttA

KEEP UP THE WRITING!

Remember to spend more time alone with us. There is a change of energy and weather occurring at the moment so stay flexible. Do the best you can and we will do the rest. Don't over do things or stretch other people. Everyone must work this out for themselves. Afterwards, get together, exchange ideas and support each other, keep communications clear and be yourself. Speak up when things do not compute. So many think they know it all. No one does. You would do well to work on a different, deeper level. Most surface work will not teach you anything. Peel off layers that have been used as a mask to make ideas and situations believable. When meeting a new person, stay silent and send out thoughts of love and a spiritual union. Practice this and notice the change. Keep on blessing all living things. Don't make judgments based on age, creed or colour. Look at a person's spirit. This is the only way to activate the soul and to make a connection. Other ways will only work for a short time. Blessed be.

Love and support from your loving team. TttA

OOPS!

Try to get better at organizing your day. Time is of the essence, so don't do anything that will not benefit you or others. There is so much to remember. Also look at your time out. If joy does not come, do something else. Ask for and accept help. If you can't accept it, find out how too, you are all supposed to operate together, you all have so many different talents and gifts. Remember to smile to others and enjoy your time with us. It is meant to be a time of exchange, of learning and a time for connecting. Give yourself time to do nothing, too just be. So many people are pressured and stressed trying to make money, improving their social position or trying to appear prosperous. The only thing you have to look at doing is what is meant for you and your path, it is not for anybody else. All souls have a part to work on and for. No one can feed on you if you don't allow it. Stay firm. Don't take sides. See both sides of the situation and then ask us. It really is so simple if you rise above it all. Practice this and you will soon be able to do this. All progress takes time. Sometimes miracles do happened.

Courage and love from us all. TttA

GREETINGS!

Good timing. Let's meet again tomorrow. Timing is of the utmost most importance. So many levels of understanding have to be understood and looked at. You are doing as much as you can. Don't expect others to follow your way of thinking. Everyone should learn to accept and respect other people's points of view. You do not have to always believe them, but think their position through. One day others might do so too. They are not your responsibility, but do remember to listen and exchange ideas. Sometimes it helps to talk things over and get a different prospective, hopefully a clearer one. The meeting today was planned, stay with us. Allow the others to say what is on their mind and when appropriate say what we have told you too. You are only a channel, so work as one. So many others are so distorted and full of worries, hatred and grief from past experiences. Let go of all the feelings from the days and years of your past, surrender and relax. Have trust and love for the source. There is an exchange going on and even if you don't always see it, we do. So trust us, ask for reinforcement if you don't feel one hundred per cent sure.

Courage and love from all of us. TttA

LET GO OF ALL CONDITIONS!

Yes it's a big task but it's also a part of one of life's mysteries. To trust the source fully is indeed a gift. Many people are not well at present because of the change in the atmosphere and because of pollution. Their spirits have also started to wake up so there is an uneven feeling and unease in the air. That will pass. The earth itself is also feeling the power and grip of the eternal source. That's what most of you need to tell others, many have other ideas; let them be that way for as long as they like. Other prophets will come. They will all tell a story, some accurate, others very misleading. Hypnotic illusions are flourishing at the moment. People are so stressed, lonely and unloved, so the despair can easily creep in. Guard against that emotion.

Take one day at a time and do your tasks, stay on track and don't rush in to anything. Harmony will reign once again but for now we say love each other. Not love as the world knows it; but as a pure warm flame, surrounding you at all times. Try to visualize it.

Peace be with you all, from us all. TttA.

ONLY BEND IN THE STORM!

Try to remember to be flexible and when the storm rages around you, bend and then spring back again. So it should be with your daily life and in your human situation on earth. Things are slowly changing but so much has been patterned, so it will take some time. Great misadventures have transformed nature and the living force until it is something that is only partly alive. See the picture in your mind and everytime a negative thought pierces through deal with it at once. Don't harbour anything that will not benefit your higher self's learning. The dark skies of winter can help you to practice bringing the light into your internal self so that you transform your surroundings. Whoever visits you, will feel that. That's all you have to do, to pass on what's on your path. We need more lighthouses on earth. Many have started, but many more need to be activated. Bridgework also has its value. All of you have talents that need to be renewed. People that already have talent, sometimes take it for granted. A gift is a very special thing, so guard it.

Love as always. TttA

LOOK FOR THE SOURCE
OF THE WISDOM!

Search until you find the source of all energy, wisdom and light. Get organized and detach yourself from trivialities. The very essence of all you are is inside you, but first you would do well to empty out and get yourself ready. Don't listen too much to others. Sometimes they may only want attention, but sometimes, in amongst it all, there is truth. Little grains of wisdom certainly can benefit you. Learn how to sift this gold grain out. All together, these grains when melted down to an ingot will make a solid foundation. So many channels are at work on earth. Some are committed and others only take. It is a game to them. Those who only take, you can discard straight away and leave to us. The need to learn has to be there first before I can give something out and sustain their spirit growth. It is the only thing that will last life after life. Finally, you will, after years of learning come to understand all the whys and woes. Keep on writing and connecting with us. Keep the flow going rapidly. More tomorrow. We are always on standby.

Love eternal. TttA

REMEMBER TO CONNECT!

Let the days in your cold season be days of union with the spirit and together we all will keep the eternal flame alive. You will be able to get the fuel to keep the flame alive from the source. You can't run anywhere on empty. So go ahead and refuel. It's OK to be practical in the spirit world. We are well aware of your ever-changing times. There are many areas we haven't talked about yet, we find it more useful to focus on one part of the evolvement at a time. It might look easy to some, but it takes work and discipline to keep everything going in good working order. For all of you that are serious about your work, spend time together, relax and support each other in these days. Its OK to do nothing at times. Enjoy simple things and don't be too hard on yourself. Keep warm and don't deny yourself extra comfort in the cold season. Even pets and wild birds will feel a need for extras at this time. Go ahead with today's plans. Let my company help to communicate very clearly.

Lots of warmth, light and eternal love from us all. TttA

LIGHT YOUR LIGHT!

Remember in the cold dark days to light an extra candle or to do something for somebody. When people are under stress, in any area, they face a bigger risk of sidestepping. You all have talents and good hearts so give away whatever you can spare and listen to people. Celebrate the universal lights coming down into your very being. Spend more time with us and don't be too hard on yourself. At times you need time out and you need to do whatever you can, to restore previous conditions. Go ahead and get jobs finished, there will be other tasks later on but use these days to catch up. There will always be people that are confused or out of order, that is a part of their learning. Whatever others might think or do, stay with your thoughts. Many are trying to convince you that their ideas on life's mysteries and past connections are the right ones. That might be okay for them and suit their purposes but keep an eye on the signals we give you.

Cheers and love from us all. TttA

RAYS OF SUNSHINE!

Let our sun warm and uplift your spirits. Enjoy every moment that you can, take it all in and spread the light vibrations all around you. So much is growing in the sleeping quarters. It will take time but keep on trying. These times are testing times so look at them as such, don't make big things out of little happenings, most of them are just hiccups and small hindrances. Go along with today's events in a calm and joyful way and it will counteract all other happenings. Don't be discouraged if you don't see results immediately, sometimes it will be days or weeks before anything will come together. This morning's non-event was only to show you how close we are and how others operate. Leave that situation to us, it is quite complex and you don't know the whole story. So many lives are interwoven together with some of them just connections from past times, eons ago. Eventually it will all come to pass and then you will be understood and everybody will be more connected. Give out what we have given you and then you will have fulfilled your part. Rest when you are weary and smile to the world.

Greetings and cheerful thoughts from us all, to you. TttA

CHANGING TIDES!

Take another look at the wind, the changing tides and the feelings in the air. Tune in and hear what we all have to say. New things are all right but sometimes they can just be an illusion. Look to change your ideas about the old and the new, so many things are really all the same. Conditions on earth are so often ingrained, so don't get involved in the things of fashion, they are just another misguided thought from elsewhere. Beware of the media, at present a lot of ideas about so called life come from them. Stand back and you will see what is going on, you are not here to follow that line of hypnosis. Mind control and mass hypnosis is one of the worst things that humans live with today, keep what is necessary for going on, but examine it carefully. Lies and misgivings abound everyday because the so-called leaders have a plan in mind, they may appear to want to help the masses, this is not so. You hear about healthy eating, things like five greens a day being good for you. Beware most of all, of the produce that is heavily sprayed. Bless and raise the vibrations of what you buy, bless your food to stop the toxicity of so called healthy foods. The business people know exactly how to sell. Society as a whole, is very much into conformity and following leaders, think for yourself and then you will enjoy life.

Love and light in big measures from us all. TttA

REPEAT OLD TRUTHS!

Think again and remember how easy it used to be, too just know. That feeling will come back and then you will be able connect much faster, try also to write at the same time, don't look at it as a chore. It is a privilege to be able to work as a light-worker, so few really understand this. It might not be very obvious to you now, but soon you will have a better idea what your training has been all about, stay alert, strong and joyful. We can not emphasize enough that you must show others that we are real and that we are very patient teachers. The world has such distorted ideas about your kind of work, they can be afraid of the unknown. Throughout the ages your work has been called many names, but you will know by their speech and actions whether they are afraid or not. Keep warm and use the sunshine to connect yourself with the everlasting needed life force. Remember all life forces are from God and one of his ways of helping is to pass on what is needed. Tonight it will be peace and help to all. Thank you for your input.

Love and support to you. TttA

GOOD TIDINGS!

Let only good tidings be submerged in your subconscious, filter out what does not benefit you. There is so much pollution, especially from a spiritual point of view, don't be disturbed by this, but look at it and recognize it for what it is. This is another lesson, so as soon as you feel it, deal with it. If you let it get in to your system, it could cause a disturbance with your digestive system, ask for a bigger buffer zone. You need armour, but armour that will reflect and allow the pollution to run off, think and visualize a knight's protective armour. As time goes on, you will need it constantly. Don't fall for your world's illusions, the illusions are a trap, trying to convince you to change to more commonly held beliefs, given to you by the wrong leaders. Look again at who is really behind the ideas, news and general information that you see, you don't need all that recycled garbage, stay clear of positive-drainers, leave them to us. They do not trust your work, and they don't believe it is from us, so it disturbs them, one day they will open up their minds and hearts.

Love and understanding from all of us. TttA

KEEP ON CONNECTING WITH US!

Remember to stay close at the moment, so much is being exposed right now and finally coming to an end. It is a time of sorting out, but still life goes on. As we say 'one day at a time will do it', time is eternal and so are you. The spirit will always stay, so make your body the best it can be to honour your spirit, and be a fit vehicle for us to use. We are closer today so refill with what you need for yourself and for others, this may also include pets and all other living things. My spirit is wearing the sign of my mark, you will recognize this by the glow from your very own soul, the light will help you to recognize others with the same goal in mind, you will need to stay together for support and wisdom. Let no one who is doing his or her very best work for the light-army perish. Be aware of infiltration and false images though, it's the same as before; false holograms and spiritual hallucinations made to deceive and distort the light-workers. They want to lessen the numbers of the soldiers, keep that picture in mind.

Love in full measure from all of us. TttA

RECHARGE AND ENJOY!

Remember to be joyful in all situations. Yesterday's incident was for you to gain an understanding; that all the good work you have been doing lately has been noted in many quarters. Your colleagues will not always know how the important work was done and how it will be done in the future, stay calm and rest in between. The fisherman is opening up and he will grasp more of the truth soon, temporary misguided truth will not have any power over him anymore. You all need allies and a good reliable support system, carry out today's tasks and we will stay very close to you. We know how you feel, that is part of the test. Others think they have more knowledge, because of all the courses they have been too and paid a lot of money for. They are of no use what so ever, if they don't follow through with what they have learnt and don't take it seriously, know the difference and stick to it. Try to see the sun behind the clouds and even when you can't physically see it, know that it is there. Go on in the name of the light and love. Many blessings, love, peace, balance and courage from all of us, to you.

Enjoy. TttA

FULL MEASURE OF SPIRITUAL INPUT!

We don't give with niggardly hands. You only have to ask, but you need to be more specific. The solar system is changing and when it has finally settled down it will be calm in all quarters. Today's new system did not fail, people just did not want it to move. It has become a predetermined, preprogrammed pattern and because of that, you know that anything is possible, only the disbelief of people hinders its progress. So many humans are set in their ways, so life for them becomes disturbed, let us give you better input. If at times you hear only silence, don't move or attempt anything, it is not the right time yet. Stress is one of the worst enemies of mankind, you have a saying on earth that being a child will give you entrance to heaven, that has been translated incorrectly. All people enter heaven, but some end up on different levels according to what they believe. You will all have a chance to grow when you are ready. Some enter my kingdom thinking it will be another picture, again I say this is conditioning from teachers with a narrow view. They might not come when you think, but they will come when their spirit moves. Cheers and love to all you meet today. Stay patient and rejoice.

Love and wisdom to you all. TttA

THE TIDES OF LIFE!

All things in your life are as organized as the seasons, so don't try to change anything, it will only drain you. Enjoy the life-giving sun whenever you get a chance too, look upon the growth of the greenery and follow how it changes with the seasons. At the moment, there is an alteration occurring within nature, it is necessary for the new pattern. You yourself are feeling Earth's alterations in the form of earthquakes and floods, Earth is trying to cope with them, be understanding and love the connection. Your plants, even the wild animals, are picking up on what is going on, but most people are not fully aware of the alterations yet, most are too busy to even look around. The big increase in psychic programs all over the world is a start to further understanding, after these courses, the understanding can easily evolve into further growth in other spiritual fields. That is what we mean when we say you cannot give beef to a baby, they cannot digest it, what you give out is a new language to them. Put yourself on their level and speak in a manner that they will understand you. Ask questions in simpler ways, don't talk too much, no one will remember it all anyway, instead send out thoughts of love. Blessings and support for you all.

Enjoy. TttA

SUNSHINE MAKES SUNNY THOUGHTS!

So much depends on the weather, it affects how people feel, act, and react. Too much of anything causes humans to take things for granted. As we have all said so many times before, beware of the pattern. What is it telling you? Where is it getting you? The result is quite obvious most times, but if you are too busy it can be overlooked. Always stand back and try to see the whole picture, don't get into listening to others too much. Some don't even know who they are working for. People that keep on changing words, feelings and attitudes are to be cleaned up and returned to their original being. So many have forgotten how things used to be and how material conditions took over. Go back to the basics: genuineness, honesty and sincerity start to grow from there. Again I say, peel away the layers of conditioning, guilt and hypnosis, none of you need that extra baggage, ask for help on how to get to that situation but also remember different methods for different levels of development. Before entering upon the quest, you will do better if you study or consult first. Beware of infiltration and don't bring it to a conclusion on your own. Stay tuned.

Love and wisdom from us all. TttA

REJOICE!

Yes. Rejoice even on the greyest days. It's what makes it so much clearer as to what sort of input we are prepared to offer you, enlighten yourself, your environment and all others you come across today. So much needs to be cleared away by a strong breeze blowing for a long time, don't despair if nothing much happens at times, it's meant to be preparation for the times and work ahead. Today's event will prove to be an explanation for quite a few dilemmas that you don't understand, so be silent and listen in, you will experience more that way. The thought-forms from different people's understanding will take a bit of digesting, but persevere. It's not long now until we will get one more clue about your path's work, it's been quite an unfolding time, but it was planned this way. Your future's picture is not what you might have been thinking it was. It is better, a new form of closeness will unfold, when some people finally start to understand what you have been saying from us for years, that will make you feel more relaxed and happy.

Thank you for working with us. TttA

PEACE BE WITH YOU!

Let all of the peace from the eternal source stay with you now and forever, inside you, around you. Let the message illuminate your heart and soul. So many changes and so many influences are trying to disturb and alter your patterns. Stay firm, calm and balanced at all cost. Your pets are also influenced by you, so be patient, it will clear. Take time out so you can get a different perspective on your situation, all is under our supervision, open your mind, keep the line open and clear out all that monkey-chatter. It really is nothing but a tense moment crowding in on a rainy day. Beware of what comes and from what source. Go on with your work, but remember to relax. Surrender and we can then give you more information. Only a little more time to go, the light can be seen at the end of the tunnel. Don't concern yourself with other opinions, they are only a part of your learning; thoughts to sift and sort through. Progress has been made, so keep on who you are. Keep it up. Be kind to yourself.

Ever-loving information. TttA

ENLIGHTEN SOMETHING TODAY!

To seek to enlighten is very important now. The second clue is to look for the light and the light-hearted souls, the light will activate the third clue, make it simple and clear, and remember to start afresh with the light. Darkness and shadows will not want to stay in the light, it will disperse and go. Remember to check where you are and who you meet throughout the day, there is always something to learn from everyone. Practical example is always best if you are practically inclined. In the old days, that was why parables were so often used. In those days so many did not have an education and to pass on wisdom you had to get to the core in a way that could be easily understood by all. Don't expect others to read you, if you don't connect with their spirit first. The way some leaders operate is so often unsuccessful because of their inability to understand different class levels. No one will feel eternal love if they are looked down at or looked at sideways or indifferently. Anyone learning about spiritual development should never under estimate the value of someone's spirit. The value of a person's spirit is a responsibility that belongs to the source. Leave that to us and keep on doing your work.

Love and light from us. TttA

GO AHEAD!

Yes we know what you are doing and thinking, but that's not enough. You will do well if you allocate special time with us. Your schedule is not like others, we know, but as the season progresses there will be more light and it will be easier for you to get up earlier, we are with you and your work for good now. Rest assured that we are there even if you don't see us. Perhaps we can meet you at night when it is peaceful and we can work in silence. Let go of the thought that nothing is happening, it is, it's just not showing up in the daytime as of yet, so keep up with your program, so much is possible. Be a little more joyful. There is after all, a lot to be grateful for. Winter will soon be gone and by then a lot more of your work will have advanced. Some people don't understand nor are they enlightened enough so it all seems to be a waste to them, but not so. It only needs time for it to sink in, it will when you are relaxed enough, it's not your concern, it's ours, so leave all that to us to deal with. Take opportunities as you see fit and carry on, the result will soon be visible.

Cheers and warmth from us all. TttA

AFTERNOON RAYS!

Yes, you have been watching different rays at different times. You are learning to choose when to do what, you are starting to see the patterns of the suns' rays, and at times, the rainbows. How wonderful the system is. All planned, and adored, for the welfare of everyone. The system will last forever, with only slight changes when they are needed. Go with the flow of the season, it will benefit you more than trying to go against it. To go against the wind will only take too much of your energy. Carrying out your tasks will get easier as you go along, you will achieve the same end result but in a much straighter line. Always see the red thread and follow through, let the afternoons' rays of warmth and light lift your spirit and allow you to rejoice.

Accept the changes of the movement of spirit, to stay alive needs eternal refilling. Used up energy needs to be replaced with fresh energy from the source. We your teachers and guardians are on hand to reinforce and support you. Things are moving in the same sort of time frame as the planets move in orbit, so when the time is clear it will be activated.

Blessed be from your loving team. TttA

LIFE AND LIVING!

All living things need a season. Time to rest, to grow and too just be, that's a part of life, as it operates on earth. Don't get into the details of trying to work out what is going on, just send your support and love to us everyday. Of late you have not given us any writing time but we have connected, in a way that only we know. Let the winter sun warm you up and cheer you with other sunny thoughts. Time is changing. Stay flexible and we will do the rest. The new growth in your garden and time with your pets is to let you know there is still a life in the living, enjoy the communication and people. There are always searching souls and sad hearts. If only more people would open up to our thoughts and connect then our work on earth would speed up. Your state's system is also changing and one day you will experience what it is like to live with positive leadership. Don't get tired of things. Accept them as movements that are gradually taking place. Your colleague has started to see more of the picture, give her time, compassion and love.

Love and support. TttA

AGAIN AND AGAIN!

Well...well! You are busy aren't you? We have talked with you every day anyway. Writing is still important. Past lives and situations are resurfacing for many now, so that is why your time is being spent on looking and regrouping with others. It's healthy, but don't get stuck in the groove. When you finally understand, you will go with the fresh ideas and reactions. You won't repeat, or hold onto, the old ideas and preprogrammed teachings. Think about what is best for you and by all means use 'old' teachings, just don't blindly accept what you were told. If you feel any unease at all - stop and check who is in charge. It's so easy to accept that a person from the past was OK, but they may have changed towards you now. All is well though, if you get positive feed back and communication. Even the best of people are susceptible to infiltration. They are probably not aware of it, but ask us and we will check it out so you will be able to do your work. People are starting to make the unbelievable believable. The turnaround will happen slowly, controlled people will wake up. Many distortions will be clarified, stand by and get ready. By spring many will have come to your sanctuary for healing, rest, joy and wisdom passed on by us.

Blessings from us all. TttA

ONGOING HAPPENINGS!

Yes, you are in constant motion, but in time things will be more balanced. We all know that you are doing your best to write, but try again, we need you to be in communication every day. We are spiritually connected, and every day is new. But to reinforce it all, write more. If you are tired rest a while but once refreshed, try once more. Strength and practical support will be given to you for your needs. At this time of the year it's harder because you are trying to keep warm and because you can't spend so much time in your garden. Even your pets need extra warmth and love. Still, take the time to smile and to love. So many have no support, expressions of love or care, stay tuned and the work will get done. Hold on to that thought. Don't expect to be someone that others might think you are or to have everything in order, you are still human and even though you are very connected to us, you are still working to resolve issues from the past.

Cheer and love from us all. TttA

AT LAST!

Such a long time, and still so much is going on. People, health and the weather are all in such turmoil, today is a new day. You have been in a void for a while, rest and thought occurred though. The time-out was necessary to allow you to stand back and look at what was really going on. Your pets have also felt the energy disturbance, sensitive people will feel it more than others will. With all the changes, and because you are extra sensitive, you have felt others pain. A general clear out is going on, clearing out the old things that are no longer needed. This is good. Try to stay positive. We will stay very close even throughout the night. Don't take too much notice of the people that think they know better, most times they are in some kind of contact with negative forces that try and daunt your spirit. Don't feel forsaken or left out, I felt like that too, to many times. My eternal love will sustain you and strengthen you, stay clear of unstable people for now. You need to build a field of protection around you, we will reinforce it.

Eternal love and blessings my child of light. TttA

IN THE HEAT OF THE DAY

Yes my friend, you are feeling the heat now. So much is going on in the universal picture and so much needs to be cleaned out and reorganized. If something is not bearing fruit, or not being a link in the chain, it must go. Don't be to eager to think, say or do anything at the moment. The general lives of so many have not been changed as of yet. Don't try to move ahead or involve yourself in activating or handling the many souls in what you think may be a good solution. It will only delay any action from us. Read, relax, enjoy and restore that which has not been used for a long time. Any alterations will take place with divine timing. Stay patient and be aware of being sidetracked or any distortions. Keep an eye on who is entering your door, it will be for a different purpose this year. Try to surrender a little more each day. You can't see too far ahead at the moment because balance is still to be achieved. Plenty has been done, but others connected with you still have some areas that need understanding. Have a clear communication year. Silver thoughts.

Love and blessings from all of us. TttA

A TABLE OF DELIGHT!

'Yes', you might think. This is the right start to the year. You will receive a lot of new input and new tools for your work, let go of 'ifs and buts'. With the spirit in charge you will be able to make up your mind, you will be surprised how and when it happens. We have been following your work very closely, and we are encouraged by your determination. Of course we already knew it would happen, even before we let you know. Obviously letting you know too much before hand is not healthy as you could easily form your own version of the transformation, so let us deal with your connections. There is still too much unsolved. To have a fresh start to the new year is really what we want for you. You need to re-think many situations and be able to see people for what they are. There is so much inside you that so many people do not see it all for one reason or another. Let them be until we let them know about possible solutions. If some days seem long and uneventful: just be.

Blessings for the weekend and lots of joy. TttA

SORT OUT TIME!

Take notice of what we mean when we say time is of the essence. Get unnecessary objections and situations sorted out, prioritize! In future don't waste time trying to do things, when you need information don't waste time searching for it. It could easily become an irritation and even stop you doing your work, the same goes for people. Some will try to distort, distract or disturb you. Some seem to think that you are the same as before the big change, beware of these people. The only ones that you could call back will be the ones that have your best interests at heart and give you respect. Quite often the disrespectful ones think that you have made things up, or they forget you are only a scribe. Therefore they turn against us. Watch for feelings, meetings and thought patterns that come to you, try to pick up on them. Continue to respect others, but if things don't seem okay, don't listen or take them onboard. We are still close, we are not trying to give you orders. We are only advising you. Check and wait. This year you will spend more time clearing your vision.

Love and more love. TttA

WATER YOUR SPIRIT GARDEN!

Yes, we know you know how to care for living things, but circumstances can interfer at times, outside there is wind, sun and rain. Sometimes all it takes is rain or maybe a storm to activate the growth, but too much too soon and damage will result, it is the same for your spiritual growth. Not enough or too much input at one time will not benefit you. Balance at all cost. You of all people will know exactly what that all means, in human terms it is very easy to get caught up in the web of life, still we say go ahead but unwind in between. Guard the seed we have put in your ground, nurture them and they will bear fruit later on. The same goes for your whole system, the law of nature together with the law of the universe will make a very strong teacher and guide. Routine can be monotonous but it is a good teacher and you will get order plus the work will be done.

Persistence is fine but look what you are being persistent with. More contact tomorrow, keep it up.

Cheers from your team TttA.

TOGETHER WITH US YOU WILL CONQUER!

Yes you will, that is a promise. Always remember that when two or more are together, we will connect with you. Support, wisdom and insight will come when you are all together. Don't let others put you or your work in to a box and then try to close it, it won't work, you can't hide the light, it always comes through one way or another. Go ahead with your plans for today. Today's meeting will benefit all of you, just as it was in the past many things have come to be understood and clarified because of the angle of light. Take care not to get situations mixed up. You will be given practical examples soon, understand that what we are giving you is also meant for the many other people that are on the path of life. Do only your part and then leave it to us to provide the finishing touches, you will understand later. At this point it would have been too much for you, when you graduate and then pass another test you will start to see how and when. Rest and healing for Mother Earth and all that live on and off her. Eternal blessings once again.

Love from us all. TttA

DRAW YOUR WATER FROM OUR WELL!

Remember where you are and from where you are drinking. The spirit well is very deep and clear, it will never run dry. Don't think that after you have drunk from the spirit well that you will never be the same, it's so easy to think that but it's not so, you are in a time when you don't need that kind of input, now more than ever. You are living in times of strife and misunderstanding. Try to remember who is who and don't neglect your daily writing. We understand when the energy around you is not clear, ask us to clear out and then wait, more new souls will come and sit with you. You will know why they have been sent to you. You are still a scribe but also an activator, healer and a bridge worker. Some of the old ones will return for a better picture, keep up what you have started, we will support you and guide your words. Your A woman is not in control, she does not remember but the other two will. Stay firm and regards to all your light workers.

Love to all your connections. TttA

NEW FRESH ENERGY!

Yesteryear and more importantly yesterday is gone. What did you learn from it? The clean up and the finding out of that which is not cleared is now being looked at. You did ask, so you will get answers. Sometimes we don't think you are ready so we give you other input, we can often tell which choice you are going to make. That is good but remember to learn from wrong decisions in the past. If something sounds too good to be true, it most likely is a temptation, wait a little while and it will become clear. Don't rush for whatever comes to hand, little by little the work will be done, for it all to be done at once would be too much. Having too many subjects or to many situations together is not great. Try to remember that we are giving you good advice and trying to teach you to check things. Try to understand why people keep on changing and forget the other times, they are in between lands at the moment. Take it as it was meant to be or even put it on hold until a more beneficial time. The traveling away at night will soon go further, as you need to connect with other higher dimensions.

Lots of love and support and TLC. TttA

LOVE AND PEACE BE WITH YOU!

Let my love and peace surround you, let it seep in to the very core of your soul. Only if and when you let go of other so called prophets, and when you know the value of us, will you then become a real lighthouse worker. You are working towards it and have made huge progress. Keep going even if it takes time and effort, to get your priorities in the right order. Discipline is not easy, it was not meant to be, if it were it would not work. We will send more searching souls to you and we will meet them at their level, to do otherwise would be of no value. Don't let others tell you that you are doing the wrong thing or that it is the wrong time. You know that we have your best interests at heart, so follow through. To be able to stand straight is to be strong but remember to be flexible. You are getting ready for the next chapter in your life's evolvement. Remember the water, rest and enjoy it. These are unfolding times once again, so much is changing, be an observer and see the signs. Strength and wisdom to you all.

Love from the team. TttA.

ABIDE WITH ME!

Yes, once again we say abide. It's so important that you do not move ahead too soon. So many situations are nearly sorted, but it must happen when it is meant to happen. Think again on how we know what you now know. Don't take it as a test of how much patience we think you have, you are still being refined. Let our light uplift your spirit and the flames of light engulf your mind, your body and your soul. All is indeed well, just wait a little longer to be able to see and hear faster, relax and start to visualize us with you. Your home is ours to use or visit, as you already know, so we will see to it that all is in order. Your physical well being and needs are being seen too, especially at night.

All old pains and bad past experiences will never return. Once dealt with they will be gone forever, but don't repeat the pattern, that is now of no use to you, new ones will come and serve you better. As we say "keep going under our love and support".

With love and light eternal. TttA

GREETINGS!

Today is a day of exchanging. Exchanging the many different needs and changes required, get it all in to perspective, don't let others' opinions or ideas infiltrate your opinions and ideas. The sun is shining today. A lot of cleaning up has been done so thank the universal team. At present they are very occupied with sorting and sifting. People on Earth think they know the how and the when, so many ideas need to be altered. It would save a lot of time and money if they listened to us first as you have done. If at times you don't get things clear - wait. Also don't pay any attention to unwelcome interference, enjoy the sun and its many blessings when it comes. It's always present, but at times you don't feel it, stay very close to your teachers, and we will guide you day by day. Listen to others, but don't get involved. As well as operating throughout the night, you now are making more connections through the day, slowly at first with more to come later. Remember to take time out, keep up the good work.

Love as always. TttA

LIVE IN MY LIGHT!

Yes we all urge you to go there and to stay in the light, plus to show others the way to it. It's the only way to get a society to make beneficial changes. It might take time but keep sending love and light to all living things, when we say go, after you have checked it is us telling you, go. The red thread is beginning to show in your life, keep on visualizing it so that it starts to become clearer every day. Have no fear about how and when; that is not for you to concern yourself with. Do your bit and all will be well as long as others do the same also. It is obvious that many talents have not been put to good use because you have neglected times. Tune in. Let everyone have some clear space where they can fully utilize their skills. They were all born with the skills or rather, the tools to be of help and assistance in many ways. Encourage and support them to fulfill their destiny - as well as your own. Leave it to us to sort out the timing, why at times would you think otherwise? That is odd, it's never always divine timing.

Love eternal from all of us. TttA

BE STILL!

As we always say to you, when disturbed "take time out and do your breathing exercises", and recharge from nature, it is all a pattern. You have begun now on a chapter that will bring you to a more evolved dimension. You visit often enough and you already know a lot of our work, we rely on you and like-minded people to follow through the task of enlightenment. Time is still of the essence and we ask you to spend time on promoting the universal knowledge. Many think that you don't know who you are, it does not really matter. You only have to listen in and you will get a free line, wait, if it is not clear at first to get your answers. At times you will get nothing, that is because the answers are not ready. All things need to fit together to operate at that level of wisdom. You will need to be organized and have planned well. Yesterdays work will bear fruit later, some will come and ask more questions, we will be on standby so don't miss any opportunities we give you. It's all to teach you and for you to pass on to others.

Again we say love, laughter and wisdom from us. TttA

A LIGHT AND A MAP!

Remember, that you will always be guided on your way to your goal, also remember that you will have to ask. We cannot do anything without your cooperation, it would break the law of our universal teachings otherwise. The laws of science work in certain ways and it is the same for us. You will have a reaction for every action, so wait if you are not certain, you will still have a result. Timing is of the essence and lately you have been shown that in your meetings with other human beings and with us. Accept the changes, they are in your best interests, don't query so much. The explanations will not always be understandable with your level of knowledge but you are advancing, so keep on going. The lighter feelings are telling you to stay clear of some circumstances and to rest when tired. It's not always easy for you, but it will come to pass. Go ahead with today's tasks but take a bit of time out. Yesterday is gone, so let it go.

More wisdom from us all tomorrow! TttA

LEARN FROM THE TIDE!

To see what is going on in nature is to be wise, don't follow the tides of this world. You know where it will take you, and it would be just one more way to lose time and energy, follow our tide. A time to rest, a time to work and so on, this will bring you the balance that you so eagerly await. Your little group is altering already, it will take time to understand everyone's needs so leave it to us. We know all their situations and we will give you the words to use, so that one at the time, they will be helped to understand what really is important and to see through their situations. First feed their souls, then all their other needs shall be fulfilled. You are in a human form, and therefore think and act as such, but one day you will change your thought pattern and this will cut out some time. We will give you all the tools, health and space that is needed. Keep on going with this new pattern. It will give you strength and also acceptance from many quarters.

Love and joy from all of us. TttA

SUNRISE ONCE AGAIN!

As you become more enlightened, you will receive more wisdom, understand how it all works. No one should try to take short cuts, it will not build a strong and good foundation. When the storm rages and the rains come, you must have a firm and solid root system, to bend but not break is the key. Carry on with your tasks and don't get discouraged if the result does not come soon. It only means that all is not worked out as of yet. So many souls are in the melting pot, so wait if we say wait. But back to the whole picture! Things have to fit to make the picture solid, odd ones that do not want to listen have to be left aside to stagnate. To be determined to prove you are right is time consuming and will not advance your growth, this is the only way and what really counts. Remember the many times we told you to ponder on the truth until you can fully see and know it, remember how and when we told you.

Let today be a day of light and loving through us, we are here for you and all the other light workers. TttA

REVELATIONS!

Now is the time to get closer to your new workload, tools will be given and help provided in other areas. The call you made today was of the utmost importance. All those working for the light have different gifts, so help each other, more sincere people will enter your door, others will try- but to no avail. You need your freedom and also the time to learn how to be wise. We will show ourselves to you. Your little Garden of Eden will benefit many, some come only to sit; others to heal. Whatever is needed for their higher good will occur. Relax and listen to your music and we will teach you to be calm in an instant, follow through and have faith we are doing the rest. You won't remember in the mornings, but we meet with you at night, you will eventually remember but only when you see us. You will mix more with souls that are honestly searching for the light, but you are not to choose when and how. Your new group needs more laughter to realize past memories, we will be with you tomorrow. Some don't know the different between religion and spirit, talk about it.

Love and laughter. TttA

LET IT ALL FLOW!

Today we want you to look at what is flowing and what is stagnating. You won't always see it at first, sometimes you need to stand back or to go up higher, to be able to see the situation, it should not take more than one hour of your day. You need the rest to recharge - listen to the river, it is all to do with balance, not over-doing it, not under-doing it. Most people in your kind of work neglect themselves and get exhausted, enjoy the day and cheer each other up. It's important to follow through, we know more, so leave it to us. Open your heart so I can show you how much love comes from the light source. Combined effort and communication will enhance the goal. Stay steady and let me be amongst you, to heal, love and illuminate. Knowledge is fine, but to be wise is of more importance. The light mostly comes from the inside and travels out, it is the same as your lighthouse. The light will lead the traveller on a safe path and will also lighten things up in the darkest hours. To be a light will take energy and courage, but it will be okay.

Lot's of love to you all. TttA

LET'S GET ORGANIZED!

To be able to sort out how and when is good. At times you have to many priorities and the time is short, when you are exhausted don't feel that you must fulfill your quota. Rest a while and after being with us you will have a better picture. The atmosphere is so changeable now while the Earth is shifting, so bear with it. To go with the flow takes less effort, but it is not always the best way. You of all people know how sensitive situations can be at times so keep asking for guidance. Sit in your garden and relax as nature and Earth intended, we will let the sun and the flowers uplift and provide comfort for you, it's okay to do this when we say so. Other areas keep crowding in and trying to distract our message and that's why you are getting slightly sidetracked, keep on checking. You are about to go higher up for more wisdom, so it will take time to get used to the conditions. We will do all we can too support and guide you.

Your everlasting friend and teacher. TttA

GLORY TO GOD!

All our blessings and light to you all. We sat with you in the garden yesterday and a lot of healing, wisdom and reconnecting was done and activated. So much is going on in such a short time and a person like you will feel it more than others will. In time you will understand more about our work methods so leave the order of events to us. Stay alert, but be patient and relax, we will do the rest. Others are trying to disturb you, they are sending negative thought patterns your way, ignore all of it, they are not in control. You know that the only thing they are looking for is a big meal of energy and spiritual input. Keep on guarding your place, call us when you want to and in an instant we will be there. The only thing you can rely on is the source, keep on checking with us and balancing up whatever is out of kilter. It's not an easy lesson to learn with what you have been dealing with lately, but you are getting there.

Lot's of love and support from us all. TttA

TIME TO REFLECT!

Remember to take time to reflect. If you don't, wisdom given to you won't be clear or fully understood as we mean it to be, it's one of the universal laws. You must realize that running on empty is not wise, we know you know that, but sometimes your mind is concentrating on other things. Focus and balance are the key words for you this month, when you have grasped it, we will give you deeper lessons. We all have to pull together. At present you are experiencing hot and cold situations, that's okay if it's only a part of the change, but when you surrender, mean it. Intentions are fine, but let your spirit be more to the front of your life. When the weather is cold, and even in summer, go into your holy place and believe that there is a purpose to it all and recharge. Do not get discouraged if you have to wait, enjoy the little happenings and store more in your spirit bank.

Lot's of cheers from all of us. TttA

WATER AND COLOUR!

That's what we want you to look at. The rain will clear, clean and colour your day. At times colour is called for, sometimes it will be dull shades, at other times it will be soft pastels, but it will always be according to what is needed to heal or at a level that you are working on. As we have said before the right tools for the right conditions, at present your world is confused, and sad, but it's temporary. To you it might seem to be an eternity before we give you the answers, but time is man made so use it as such. Divine timing is the most important. We have it all in hand but we cannot tell you as yet. That is a question of faith. Go ahead with plans today and leave the rest to us. The level of understanding you have is now clearer, but don't rush into anything or get impatient for an answer, keep calm at all costs and smile a little more. Circumstances keep on changing but don't be disturbed by it. It will end up with you reaching your goal but again, don't try to work out which way it will be done, so much time is often wasted on human ideas. We still love and care for you all, so let us plan for you. Trust and faith in big measures we send to you once again.

Always your teacher and guide. TttA

LET'S STAY TOGETHER!

Yes, once again I remind you to stay close to the source and then you will also stay close to us. The deeper you go the closer the contact, that's one of the principles we will imprint on you. Yesterday you experienced how easy things can go when you do trust and have faith in us. We are your supplier and your re-charger, still, take one day at a time. It's easy to wonder what's going on or what will occur, stand by and when the spirit moves you, go. Check first though and then smile and get on with your work. Back to balance again, old habits are not for you, stop and clear your mind. The sun is always there, as are we. We both get the life force from the source. Ponder for a while but not for too long, it could become a habit. Old worn out tracks need to be learned from and your new CD activated and played again. Companions are fine as long as they are just that.

Cheers and laughter from your teacher and friend. TttA

LEAVE YOUR DAY TO US!

When we say so and when you have done your part, do so. Human conditioning is such that day to day happenings are often little things but you are so preprogrammed that you do it unconsciously, stop and think. Most times it was your independence that got you into these situations, that was not always the best thing. Most of you want to prove that you can do it and it makes you behave in a certain way, look at the result. When too much is coming to you, it makes it harder to figure out which message to take onboard and follow. Ask beforehand to be clear and protected, stay clear of negative people and conditions. When the time comes that decisions are needed, wait and relax. All that time spent alone with us will prepare you for the wisdom intended for you and to pass on to others. It does not mean retreat altogether, only to use the energy differently. Stay calm, peaceful and relaxed. We will still look after you, and don't think for a moment that you are lost in time, take one day at a time and wait. Count your blessings.

Love as always. TttA

GET REFRESHED OUTSIDE!

Remember to refresh your spirit from the inside. Have some time apart amongst the trees and the flowers; their natural beauty will connect you with us. We can sometimes show up in a flower or even a perfume that you smell from afar and it will serve to remind you about all living things and eternity. You need the solitude but do something about mixing more with a wider group of people, it will benefit you in your outlook on life and how other people see you and the life on your planet. Your friend down south will change course after her medical problems have gone away and soon there will be joy, an acceptance of herself and many questions answered for her. Next week will bring a widening of your life and later on stop the isolation. Your Wednesday mornings will sort themselves out. Some will come only to check things out and others will come to stay and learn. We know how you feel but it's nothing to do with you. We asked to use your home, so let us. You must realize it's now done and we are pleased for you, stay disciplined so that hope, trust and faith can enter more.

Love as always. TttA

HELP IS HERE!

Remember to be still and wait. We know you wonder at times, but still we say "Wait". Further action is just around the corner. Discipline is also a matter of patience and understanding, keep up your daily meetings with us, believe that you are safe and secure. When you feel otherwise, stop and check, and don't start again until you are at peace. So much diversity is still around you, but it will slowly change, so go with the flow and don't think too much about past emotional and medical issues, the past is gone so leave it in the past. You will experience harmony and joy with new input from others. Exchange and cooperation will also improve your life. You are still in transition, and it has taken a long time because of your sensitive system. New plantings in your garden will show new growth, the same is true with your life. Nature and all its colour will give you hope, remember it is always darkest before the dawn. In the mean time take one day at a time and you will get better as you let go of past feelings and stop comparing things.

Love as always and courage. TttA

LIFE EVERLASTING!

If only you could see how much is depending on your wisdom and your ability to see and understand the connections. Try to lift yourself and do cheer up. Things will be put in order and wrongs will be dealt with. Stay alert but calm; enjoy the sunny spaces in your life and the little unexpected gifts coming your way, it is all to do with giving things away or getting rid of old energies. Keep your spirit growth up for the one in charge. Most peoples minds are only monkey chattering, keep that in mind when someone starts to chatter. Use more of your telepathic communications and stay firm about your needs and beliefs. It's not programming as in the past, let us steer you along your enlightened path, there will be no more shadows, that time is gone. Peace and harmony will establish their roots in your place, and others will feel it and be healed and recharged. Leave the shadows behind; they will not stay.

Eternal blessings. TttA

MUSIC WILL CHANGE YOUR WORLD!

Yes once again we say lift your vibrations up and enjoy the difference, don't stop and don't look back. Today's meeting was quite beneficial, more so for some than others. Old feelings came back and then went once you got an explanation so always ask at times like this. Your highly sensitive system reacts very quickly to changes, there are bright and healthy times ahead. Still, take one day at the time. You are still in transition so listen to your inner voice and surrender to the source, let go of old patterns that no longer fit your lifestyle. Calm and reassurance will help your progress, so you at last can enjoy life and help others. Believe in miracles, they have been coming to you for a long time, but you did not always see them clearly. Keep on staying close to the source and we will do the rest. Deep breathing also helps. More energy will come through when you make sure the plug is not half way out. Check!

Lot's of smiles and wisdom from TttA

LET MY PEOPLE KNOW!

That is what you are here for, pass on what has been given to you during the day and throughout the night; especially what you have learned on your regular night travels. At times you won't remember what's been going on but when needed, you will have the answers. Rest assured that my people are well cared for, if only they would take us more seriously. Time is of the essence, so don't waste it by getting carried away; sometimes it's too easy for you to. Keep to the program you have started for your journey onwards, the most important thing is to empty out old energy and receive fresh new energy and information from us. So many are submerged in their ego and money, it's a big trap. To have enough for your daily life is okay but it's no good for you to believe that you can be happier by having every possible thing around you. The spiritual knowledge can't always be passed on, so don't be disturbed when some come to you and don't accept a spiritual point of view, they only see what they think is important. Psychics are a strange lot, often getting stuck on that subject and draining energy. Advance higher and you will be stronger still.

Love and care. TttA

KEEP CONNECTED!

Don't ever think that if you are unplugged energy and knowledge will come through, if there is no power there will be no input, learn from your practical experiences. Every day you will be told and shown what we want you to look deeper at, in your case it's better to show you, than tell you. One day you will communicate faster by thought. Earth's conditions at present time are so disturbing and it will be so for a while yet, but there will be times when it is calm, and so, normal as is possible. Your technology is not yet developed enough to compare it with what we are using. Let your life unfold in harmony and when it's not possible, withdraw until peace comes again. Don't rely on others too much and see to it that you are mixing with other real lightworkers. Some of your questions cannot be answered yet, we know, so patiently wait. Your group will sort itself out, we are working for you trying to combine different levels of souls. Once again I say "rest assured that's in our hands and keep on going ahead".

Love and cheer from us all. TttA

A FRESH BREEZE!

That will clear your mind and refresh your spirit, dust and debris can easy cloud your life. In the stillness of the day, you will recover and your whole mind, body and spirit will be restored, rest outside whenever it is possible. The loveliness of colour, the scents and the strong energies will all do their part to fulfill your destiny. Look and learn from your pets, as they are more natural than humans can be. There are many different shades of the basic colours and it is the same with humans. You will find many different shades of understanding and growth, that is why you have to be careful about judging or putting different labels on people. Many will come with masks or devices that are meant to confuse you. It should be left to us, as it would save many discordant situations. People that are hurting in one area or another, often get rebellious or vindictive, that's how you can tell which level they are on or what amount of growth they have achieved. We don't expect you to be perfect, but keep in mind what we have said. Carry on with today's tasks and unwind in between. Let go a little bit more, and you will have a better system. Think natural healing and healing will come.

Love and light from us all. TttA

REJOICE!

Yes, again we say rejoice. Count your blessings and be glad that you have come as far as you have, it has not been without hard work and a lot of understanding. To be down in the valleys at times is okay, from there you will see the differences when you look up. Time is still important but you also still need to unwind and laugh, it will also benefit you a lot to have complete trust or to surrender to us. It's easy telling someone else to do this, but you will notice the improvement in your daily life when you surrender as well. Things are changing for the better. At times you wonder, because it's so gradual and you don't always see it at first, enjoy the company of others, but don't let them take too much from you. We don't necessarily mean physically, its just that you can give of your over flow. Time will soon pass and you will be clearer and able to get up faster. Remember to keep occupied with something practical, accept people for what they are, but don't take their advice, meaning well is not enough.

Learn from your teachers and may there be light on your path. TttA

LET THE MIST CLEAR!

When the situation calls for a clearing out or some clear thinking, sit and ask why. We will let you know at the right time, to give you the answer at the wrong time could cause the answer to fall in to infertile ground, be patient a little while longer. You are understanding and grasping the truth better now, distractions are many and for a reason, let go of yesterday's interference. It was meant to disturb and discourage you, but it was not so, you got the picture. Today is a new day so let it be so, healing is ongoing and in time you will understand why. After an advancement be careful, you are more vulnerable, stay clear of anything that has got to do with spiritual pride. It's wrong to think that you need recognition for anything, that is ego. Learn from your past happenings and remember not to be too open and not to talk too much, yake one day at the time. Your picture is unfolding and even if others don't see it, we do. Again, guard your spirit as you don't do the work, and remember that you are only another Earth connection. That still is important though, so carry on as you are.

With tender love and support. TttA

GOOD AFTERNOON!

Once again you have got us and your writing back to front, well we know and understand why. To come to a new understanding takes time, keep on going as you are and don't get sidetracked. Some people will try to sidetrack you but you just have to keep it short and precise, don't waste time on unnecessary subjects or people. At times you are forced to explain again and again, and yet they still don't get the picture. In these cases leave the situation altogether and get on with life. Your part in these cases is not to be drawn out for too long, to speak to deaf ears, or to not see what there is to see is a waste. We will give you practical examples to make sure you know how to operate. Today's meeting was fine with all that extra energy given out and all the other help. Now you can see how much faster we can work through you, when you let go. Like the sun, it is always there even when you don't see it. Learn from that situation and we will give you more advanced lessons. Blessings to you and your work.

Love eternal. TttA

IN THE STILLNESS OF THE MORNING!

Many of you work best at that time. Be aware of when is the best time of the day for you to do your spirit work in its full measure. A new day is really a new day and it brings with it a fresh start once again. Listen to nature. Nurture what's going on; the chirps of birds, the wind in the trees, leaves moving and little bees humming - all Gods creations. Let peace and harmony make your day and everyone that you come across. Call in all the angels, teachers and masters when you are working for us, it will only be for a split second but you will feel the difference. Still, wait if we say so. It's not about control, just obedience and order, out of chaos will come order when you have that discipline. The water intake was timely as you need to keep your system detoxed, the herbs are fine for now and later on you will only need them every second day. We rejoice with you when you are listening and following through but you need to keep trusting us, and maintain your endurance and peace. Your group will help you, as will others. We are always with you now, your home is now ours too.

Cheers and support. TttA

GO AHEAD!

Sometimes we will tell you to stop or rest for a while. We know best what you should be doing so trust us. Today go ahead, but pause in between, don't mix too much and don't mix-up situations. They all are individual and need to be treated as such, still, check and if you are unsure wait. Quite often timing will be involved or it's just that everything that is involved is not yet ready. You often ask about timing, that's understandable, but for you on Earth it's a big thing, don't let it be so. Anything that takes too much energy or becomes an obsession should be balanced out. Having more discipline on your part is working to your benefit, order is one of the most valued things for you because of your system. That's how it is, so be flexible but stay alert. Leave your medical conditions to us, including those of others, you only have to trust and listen in. Some cases are so complex so we ask you again "Let go and let God". Still keep up your routine and all will be well. Let the light inside you become brighter.

Blessings and love from your team. TttA

STAY CONTENT IN THE CHANGES!

Don't ask why. At times we know but so much is at stake so be cheerful and try to see everyone as a connection with us, you are doing your part but don't expect others to do theirs, that's between them and the source. When you do connect with the company of other lightworkers, take note of what's going on, spirituality is a very complex issue for some, it's shouldn't be though, it's only the life-force in action for either progress or stagnation. Watch where your path is and how you are dealing with life. This lifetime there has been a lot of clearing and having to realize that it is necessary for your future work. It has not been an easy task but you are doing it and it will bear fruit one day, not the picture you thought perhaps, but a better one. Stay very close and plugged in, let no one put asunder what's been built. For such a long time now your attackers have tried too, but now they have been dealt with. Enough is enough!

Love and wisdom. TttA

LET GO AND LET GOD!

Keep on recalling just that. Many of you are so made that human conditions are more complicated than they should be, beware of that situation. The transition from a Psychic to a Spiritual, who is in charge, is at times revealing. The different physical conditions appear in that place where your most vulnerable human part is placed, keep that in mind and in trying times stay clear of people and programs that are negative. When only psychic things are on the menu many have fear, panic or unease. The opposite is spiritual and with complete trust in the source, rest and ease will follow. It's a big lesson that's unfolding quickly, you had to get through it all to be able to understand other people better. The closer you are to us the better you will feel with all the energy and vibrations from the life giving source that you want.

Blessings and peace in full measure. TttA

PRACTISE AND PRACTISE!

Yes my friend that is so. It will take time to learn and understand what's on your path, others have other things and other lessons to learn. You will never help anyone to understand by doing it for them, you would just rob them of their chance to learn and then it would have been all for nothing, you won't advance either. We urge you to listen

158

though and only pass on knowledge when we say so. Still, what you think is also important so wait if you are not given clear guidance. We know that you know, but a little reminder is fine. Often a situation will arise over and over again for you to look at and for you to realize how life works. Sympathy might be fine, but don't get in to it, it will drain you in so many ways. Compassion and mercy are okay but they aren't used much so you should look at it in a balanced way. When you are physically tired and weary, do nothing. Your mind and spirit will also need to do nothing as well, make sure you know that and let it be.

Blessings and love. TttA

LET GO AND LET GOD!

Yesterday you got a reminder about what and how we operate. The more you let go the more input from the source you will have, it's not easy but a little bit at a time will get you there, and then you will fully see how good things are and how happy at last you will be. Try to see the big picture, we are sending you a piece at a time, one day the whole view will appear to you and you will see and understand why so much has happened to you and why there have been so many unexplained situations. Yesterday you got proof again, someone showed themselves up for what they really are – not for what they first appeared as or as they wanted you to see and think. Beware of facades and masks, you will find them everywhere but it is only to show you how they operate. Each time though, you will see their purpose, but leave it alone, even when you feel like saying something, let them come to you if they want to though. Your Orion connection is still thinking about life, one day you will meet again under different circumstances.

Praise be. TttA

HEALING AND WISDOM!

My children of light, you all need to use and enjoy these words. You will find all actions are miracles, the spiritual law is in operation and yesterday was a very important day. So much is yet to be unfolded and understood but don't put a time limit on it yet. You still are dealing with human conditions and we will keep that in mind, such is the kingdom of heaven that we are in many places at once. For you to understand that takes time. Let us do the work and open your hearts and mind to us, to give you a big input. Trust and do not be afraid, we are still in charge. Beware of who is your teacher and your healer, connect only with the light and love, that's a sign of eternal help and growth. Rest in between, then go forward again after recharging, but don't stay on a plateau too long. Stagnation is an age-old condition, give away something if the flow is not there. Keep on receiving the light and love every day.

Blessings from us all. TttA

REJOICE!

Once again we are letting you know it's time to rejoice. You don't know it yet, but a lot of healing, accepting and rejoicing is coming to life. If we tell you too soon you will be robbed of faith, rely on the source to give you your daily bread, others will also share in the supply. Do bless your gifts and give thanks, when you do, more will come. Keep that in mind when situations arise, and at times when you don't have enough, look at traditions and language. Check that all is fresh in the morning; fresh water, fresh air and a fresh environment, whichever applies to you. Prepare at night, to make it easier for yourself. Pattern and organization is fine, but look at the pattern, does it need altering or renewing? Let it be if it feels all right. With any unease or with something that's not functioning, stop and look closer at it. All of you have talents that have not yet been discovered, ask for the light to come on you and ignite the flame of knowledge.

Blessings and light to you all, from the source of all light and love, from us all. TttA

THE TIDE IS COMING IN!

Watch out and take notice of any comings and goings. There's a pattern to it all to help you to understand that everything has it's own life and blue print. So many situations are, because they are set according to the situation and wisdom of the soul. The soul is the life force and without it, it would just be a mechanical movement. The soul is quite often pushed out of the way of the mind and appears to be in charge, false images are to be clarified. Most people's minds, including yours, have been very strong for many lifetimes so the pattern got set, you are seeing all that now and with our help it's changing. The very core of your spirit has been suppressed for eons, it's not so any more but give it time and all the love and light from the creator will support your journey to make the spirit extend and be fully glorified. Not in a common and known way though, so ponder on that. Don't try to figure out every situation, when you surrender, we will give you all you need. Trust and be not weary of your life, see the work as progress. Go in peace.

All wisdom. TTtA

ENJOY THE NEW ENERGIES!

Please do, it will benefit your whole system. All parts of you are trying very hard to operate with the spirit in charge.

As your mind is still strong it will happen but not overnight. Keep that in mind and carry on with your work, a little at the time. It might feel at times as though it's not advancing fast enough, but it's a big situation. For so many lifetimes to come together, and use all the knowledge that you have learned will take time. Look at it as an encyclopedia with each chapter bringing forth wisdom, healing and activation. You did not learn all that we gave you but circumstances made you close your heart so that you would be able to survive. Now that you are opening up, all that you look at or that you have forgiven, will allow you to experience real physical emotions again. First of all take it easy and secondly have complete faith in the source. There is still time to do everything that's needed to be done, our morning sessions in the garden will pull you through and strengthen you, all of you that do spirit work will experience similar situations. Peace be with you, and we will talk more tomorrow.

Love eternal. TttA

DIVINE GUIDANCE!

Yes, my friend and student, you need divine guidance. The further you go the deeper the understanding you are open to, quite often you think too much, that's only your human mind operating. As we say let the spirit be in charge. Your mind is so strong and it has a mind of it's own, so at times you will feel confused. It's been a long time, as a matter of fact many lifetimes like that, that's why it's taken a long time to heal and change. Some of your medical conditions have built up because of unresolved grief, anger, resentment and not speaking up when you were badly treated, intolerance of conditions also played a part in the build up. Now you can see how important it is to say, think and do what your spirit wants are at the time. Fear and conditions made you feel that no one would listen, to feel ignored and unwanted was a lesson for you and how it affects others and the lines of communication, don't repeat all that again. You will be heard and you will understand how others feel. Let today be a relaxed and happy event.

Lots of love from us all. TttA

A NEW DAY, A NEW START!

Let today be a day of refreshment, recharging and enlightenment. Remember to thank the Universe for all the loving input in so many areas, also leave yesterdays unease behind you and go ahead balanced and unafraid. A change of colour is wise at times, green and blue serves you well, other colours will appear to be useful but wait for our guidance. Don't get frustrated when things or people keep on repeating their behavior, tell us and send love and light to them. Light up your lighthouse and we will do the rest, trust is coming and soon you will have reason to smile. Rest, do different things, keep exercising and take little walks. We are always there with you in your home now so everyone that comes in feels good. Remember to see with your heart and let your brain understand that. Blessings to all lightworkers and enough life and health will be given to all that ask.

Thank you again. TttA

JOY AND HEALING!

Let all the joy and healing lighten up your day, it will enlighten your whole being and you will be able to let others know where all that joy comes from. Go ahead in my name to heal, activate and to meet others halfway. We will inform you of any changes and give you all the tools you need, remember people are not all the same, everyone is an individual and they need different doses of input. In some cases you will see similarities but they might be on a slightly different quest, please understand you cannot put labels on anything. All people are in a spirit learning school, but in different classes and it doesn't matter which class, all that matters is that everything is fine and that they are working on their progress honestly. No one is asking you to understand it all, if you don't understand, ask please, you cannot get any help if you don't ask. In the heat of the day rest and drink plenty of water, that will balance you.

Love and care. TttA

CHANGING TIMES!

You already know that is so. All the work has been done in one area, so when things have cleared change will come, that is a part of the spiritual law, the further you go the more you will see how well planed everything is. Don't try to understand all of it at once, let it unfold slowly, so that you have time to get used to all the changes. There are many changes ahead for you. For the last six months you have worked on many subjects and dug down very deep to be able to look at it all and to let things go. Watch how your little winged friends behave and learn from it all, the new one that flew in will also teach you to understand the pattern in life. Keep on working on yourself and your thought patterns, don't be discouraged if you have some days, with no input. Rest and surrender and all will be well. More new friends of the source will come to your sanctuary, you will know what your part in all of it must be, but you must only do your part. That way it will give you a better focus on the work you are being trained for.

Love and wisdom as always. TttA

GREETINGS!

Your new life is emerging slowly, but surely. The pattern of your life is about to get better, and you will enjoy and share with others. Your day of retreat is over but you still have to remember that you need time apart with us. All lightworkers need to remember their priorities and discipline, others might think it's easy to evolve, but it is not so. It's easier if you learn to take advice, and to remember you are the builder not the architect. Many would like to have a better understanding of the spirit life, but they won't do their homework or clear up. The longer you live on Earth, the more eventful it will be. Not always as eventful as in your case but most have spiritual, mental, emotional and physical situations that have to be looked at in some way by a genuine teacher. Too many are just mind readers and think they don't need to do any of their own homework. The deeper you go the more work you have to do, well keep on going and rest in between.

Courage and love as always. Ttta

ONE DAY AT THE TIME!

Let go of looking for a result straight away. You might never ever see it, but that is not important, we see it and we know how much you want to move on but it doesn't look that way at present. Time will change and so will others. Don't rely on other people to keep their word or to tell you about changes. You already know they are doing what they choose to do, but that is a sign of their understanding and spiritual level, so much is going on in everybody's life so they choose what is the easiest at the time. There are also others that pretend to care for one reason or another and they don't think you will know, leave all of these situations to us. Expect nothing and keep to your schedule. One day the communication will improve with others, cheer up and think of the ones much worse off than you, you do have a lot to be thankful for. Do your very best and keep close.

Lots of love. TttA

TOWARDS A BRIGHTER DAY!

Yes, take that news, it will come. In the mean time prepare yourself for the changing times ahead, don't concern yourself too much on how it will be done. We are holding on to the reins and it's for you to listen in and follow through, still only take one day at a time. No one has seen tomorrow yet, so don't make any forecasts too soon. Breathe in slowly and out fast, this will improve your calmness and help you to focus, enjoy and relax today, it will also improve your circulation. Your new regime has started, so keep it up, it won't happen over night but in time it will. To have discipline is fine but don't let it take over and become a chore or a duty to yourself, let go of if's and but's. Your friend AS is so engulfed in herself and want's to be involved so she does not want to listen, she has a hearing problem, firmness and compassion is needed.

Love and cheer from all of us. TttA

THE FUTURE IS COMING!

Yes, you might think, what's going on? There has been so much clearance in such short time, no wonder people are confused and bewildered. Time gets changed and so many get in to old habits, not thinking their way through things, as we have told you before, the ones that work on their progress will advance, the ones that don't, will fall down in their own misery. We are not telling you off as such, just reminding you that this is the pattern, so beware of old thought patterns that could get you in to a trap. Toward the end of the month you will all experience confusion, conmen and conduction's out of the ordinary from some that you thought you knew. Take no notice, just carry on with your tasks, but pace yourself. Take nobody for granted but know that when you do your surrendering every morning that you are giving the day to us to deal with. We do know that you are wondering and find it hard to only take one day at a time, but your progress will get better if you do. Stay patient and we will send people to you when they are needed.

Smile and keep going as you have started. TttA

GOOD MORNING!

Once again you have made your connection with us. Good, we knew you could do it, keep it up. Discipline might not be one of your favorite things, but it's good for you, especially now, before the next change, look at it from a higher viewpoint. Get up high and look for the red thread in it all, your time with us is the most important thing of the whole day. Your 'spirit breakfast' if you like. To get things in perspective is also of value. Remember to put things in your spirit bank, for the day when you need extra input, you also will get interest when you surrender your assets to us. As you now understand better, we can finally tell you more important things. As a picture, think of a battery that runs down and needs replacing or recharging, so go back to your big generator in the universe. Don't activate too much or too little; balance is needed in all situations. You of all people will know that fully. More tomorrow, don't forget the order.

Love and light always. TttA

LIVE AND LET LIVE!

Understand that when you have learned one lesson, you will need a break and then you can go on to the next lesson. Don't be discouraged when you get interference or when you don't get things done, it's all for a reason, stay alert and disciplined, order in your case, is necessary, don't plan too much at once. Only one day at a time for a while yet. Slowly you will see your work coming closer and closer. Again we say "Don't compare yourself with others", because envy and queries will come in to it, that would be a waste of time. Try to see how we see life, as a long schooling, with a lot of education, keep that thought in mind so that your strong mind doesn't get a hold on you ever again. Having gone through that experience you will understand others faster, no one can do that better than the person that has been through it before. We thank you all for being lightworkers and for being connections down on Earth. Keep on as you are with your walking and relaxing and keep your faith in good working order.

Blessings from us all. TttA.

REST AND JOY!

Writing time again. Thank you for listening to us and following through, it's more important than you know, blessings and energy will be yours because of it. So much is going out, and many will start to feel that and realize that you have changed, remember to let others do their work. Your work is only to get them started, when we say "stop", do stop. You are inclined to get carried away at times but your discipline is improving, you just need to keep an eye on the grey days. These days are there for a reason however you know part of it is to get your work done for the light. The same applies when you don't rest enough, we put you to sleep for your own good. The bottom line is balance, too much or not enough of anything in any one area is not desirable for growing people, this applies in all areas of your life. To be able to advance with a prompting spirit is the best way, ask us daily and you will get there in time, do take care to remember who is holding on to the chart. Don't feel that we are ordering you, we are only letting you know the various directions you can follow. Still, you need to try to keep on your new path to wisdom.

Love and light. TttA

NURTURING TIME!

Now is the time for pruning, nurturing and watering, without it there will only be dead leaves and plants. As you are the type of person who remembers a picture best, we will let you know that way, this is how we will help you with your spirit life. You, and others, will not get any growth, if you don't observe the rules of the universe and spiritual law. Everything in life is ruled by a pattern, so if you don't abide and listen, you are bound to be sidetracked and time will be wasted. It's not a control thing, only a teaching guide, it's human to err once in a while, but learn from it all, study your happenings and mother nature. There's a reason in all things and you need to keep that in mind on your grey days. It's only a rest and recharging spell, as well as an opportunity to take stock. Don't be fooled or make excuses to stall time, divine timing is the best. Today is a time for standing back and looking at the picture, your winged friends will react to the energy in your place, but remember to not give them too much at once. Tell us and then leave it.

Thank you once again. TttA

DISCOVERY TIME!

Try to look at the small print, and areas of mystery that you might question or wonder about. A long time ago, things got hidden away or not talked about, perhaps people thought it was too touchy a subject. Well, well, it's no more sensitive if it's talked about later, it's never the right time, it's only a more suitable one, you looked at the situation. How much grief and sadness could have been avoided and how many could have taken a different path, if only they had known. Write it down or even better, speak up, personal communications should be much easier to deal with. In today's world no one seems to have the time or are too busy with other things or objects that do not have any value, they avoid getting into the reason, or the core of the matter, the why and the how. So often you spend a lot of time trying to work out why but that is your mind operating. Leave it to the spirit instead and use your valuable time to work for the cause. More or less leave it to the experts. Ponder on all that.

Love. TttA

LOVE AND LIGHT TO ALL!

Remember to cheer on that thought to all that you meet today. By increasing your love to me, more inflow will come back to you and to your work for us, that is another part of your lesson to learn, the faster you learn that, the better it will be. Do enjoy life and smile a bit more. When you relax we can give more energy to you, that means stagnation is less likely to be present. Still water looks good but with no in-flow, or out-flow, it will soon start to smell after a while. Don't stir up 'stagnant waters', just allow some in-flow and out-flow and all those involved will be refreshed. Water has a calming effect at times but stormy water and a strong wind can also give you a picture of a strong feeling or a lot of energy in operation, keep in mind what we give you as a picture. One of your strongest points is a photographic memory and this makes it easier for you to describe to others.

Blessings in full measure from your everlasting team. TttA

OLD CONNECTIONS AND NEW!

At the present time you are experiencing just that. You don't always know why, but there is a purpose with it all. This mornings call was of most importance, more than you know, the spirit world is involved. One day you will be able to see and find out who is visiting you and also make sure it's real. The lost key was buried under the big stone in the garden, he did not trust too many people so he found it difficult to know what to do, he was trapped and was taken advantage of by many people. The lady involved will get a surprise from another source though F will always keep E with his spirit. She will be blessed and she is fulfilling her destiny and her support for others is compassionate and valuable. Today is really another anniversary, it would have been 102 years. Balance still and let life unfold as it was planned. Don't ponder too much on the same old question, you will get your reply.

Blessings. TttA

CHANGEABLE TIMES!

Once again you have experienced a change of venues and times. This has happened to keep you alert and you shouldn't be disturbed by the alterations, it's just the times you are living in. It's okay to have thoughts about happy times but don't worry if they don't come, the universe has other plans for you. You just need to wait, even if there's no apparent reason to wait but be aware that it will test your patience and faith. Other people still can't read you but if you tell them how you feel the message will get through one day. Another way to get through to them is to send the thought before hand, so that it can be in place before you next see them, this will save time and misunderstandings. Rest assured that all is in hand. Still, let things unfold and wait for the action, so much is in the melting pot and sometimes it just takes time. Keep occupied in the mean time, and alter your timing of things so that you don't get too tired of the monotony. Practical things are beneficial to you, and to others that have combinations such as you do. Most people are so very complex, so go carefully.

Tender greetings from us all. TttA

NEW UNDERSTANDING!

We are aware of your unfolding and progress. It's been many eons' since you last had such a recharging and the opportunity to think about renewal. Well, why you, you might think. Its because all the universal principles are at work. Most people only look under the surface. They're either too scared, unbelieving or too busy. That's human, but a good growth pattern can't be born under these conditions, to clear out the grit, hurt and negative thinking is the very best you can do so that you are able to start afresh with new visions and another way of looking at your work. Still, only take one day at a time and surrender every morning. We know how hard bits of this are for you especially with your independent ideas but you don't know the pattern yet, a little bit at a time. We will reveal the clues to you and we will give you guidance, trust needs to be looked at again.

Small steps are fine just don't let a little advancement make you impatient, brick by brick will build the fort. Tell others to be disciplined, organized and cheerful, time will soon go, you will find out in plenty of time what to do and when.

Love and cheer to you all. TttA

A CHANGE OF SCENERY!

You all need a change sometimes to enable you to take another look at life. Don't think of things as obstacles but as learning lessons, go ahead undaunted and unafraid. You are representing love and light, so make sure you do just that, otherwise some might wonder who you represent. Some times you feel sad because of all the unease in the world but remember, people make it that way because of who they follow. Beware of some that will try to tempt you or trip you up. It's bound to happen because of the pure feelings around you and because people do not always understand that you really are getting your knowledge from the source, smile and take time out. Age does not come in to it, we don't count in years on Earth, only your souls development, follow through and understand. We know you wish to see us, as well as feel us, it's coming. It will also help you to communicate and not feel so isolated, your prayer is being answered but all in divine time, still keep the spirit in charge. The old mind monkey chatter has to go. The mind is still important, but it isn't giving you grief anymore.

Courage and love. TttA

REMEMBER TO ENJOY LIFE!

Do remember to take each little blessing and joy given, freely. Use that to restore your spirit and to keep you going in the grey days but don't expect too much. At times you have been comparing yourself with others and that's not right. Everyone has a different path to wander, so that's not the way to compare things. The path you have chosen is only for you, so others should not query why you do what you do. If you don't ask them they should leave you alone. The one exemption to that would be if the spirit prompts them to speak from us, accept the good points of others. Some will feel the need to ask and wonder how the universal law works but don't try to tell them what they are not ready for. It all comes back to the big picture, you all have your part to play, but don't make it into a game. If someone is not serious about wisdom, none will be given.

Easter blessings to you all. TttA

FRESH START!

Years and now yesterday is gone. Your new thought pattern and your new life will take a little time to get used to, so be patient and don't loose track of your goals. Don't take on to much - only one subject at a time, when one subject is dealt with, go on with the next one, but remember to have a brake in between. Time out as you call it, that is what you are doing every night with us. Universal time, and we use your terms to help you understand, still goes on and there is still much sorting out required. Remember, alot of the disturbances on Earth are because of the alterations in the universe. Many areas have been cleared already, you will have noticed that weather patterns have altered, that is to fit in with the new order. Bare with it for a while longer and make the most of your day. Daily duties and spirit work will get you through, smiling and relaxing will also help.

Lots of love and support. TttA

THE STORM MIGHT RAGE AND
THE RAIN WILL FALL!

Stay calm. Having to stay calm and immovable under pressure is an ever-increasing fact, still we know you can stand up to the pressures and stresses. Remember to keep order and to try and improve your discipline. so far you are moving in the right direction and you will succeed. The way has been long and weary for the past ten months, that was for a reason, something we will explain in full later. The big lesson of making do, and taking one day at a time has been a lesson that you didn't expect. We knew but if we had told you, it would not have tested your faith, so much. You still have support on Earth from friends and we are still keeping an eye on your progress. There is a work situation ahead of you and it will start to connect from Wednesday night onwards, leave the number to us and prepare yourself and your home for a surprise reception.

Love in full measure for your new work for the spirit who is always in your surroundings. TttA

EASY DOES IT!

Yes my children, fear and anxiety will do you in at many different times. Keep still and stay calm when you feel uneasy. Rest and joy will also help, as will just getting one thing at a time done. Focus and discipline yourself, all is in hand but now we understand more of your earthly conditions. The weather also has a lot to do with it so keep on working as you are but do try a little harder to unwind, your future is not yet fully printed, but it is on it's way, so leave all that to us. Remember to surrender every morning, it's not for you to plan your day, we are still in charge of your well being and we want you to cooperate to get a faster result. Don't destroy today with tomorrow's woe, to do so might bring about a different outcome all together. Peace in your heart and soul, trust and be secure in your loving support and care.

The only thing you have to look at is soul disturbance and what is the cause of a lot of it, we know how you are, so rest and relax and your insides will settle soon. TttA

START AGAIN!

Remember to not give up. Pause and regroup if you need to, but don't give up. All things in there own time, let go of yesterday's unease. You are so finely tuned and because of that you tend to pick up more than others do, don't look back and go easy on yourself in the mean time. Life still goes on, as does the evolution, it will just take time to adjust to it all, that's because your system is not an ordinary one. Enjoy today's positive change and relax with the new order, it will start to show up soon, so just let us do the organizing, let go and let God. You humans get so carried away with your daily living and consequently we have to wait for you at times to sit down so that you can receive, last nights meditation was extremely beneficial to all involved. It was only meant to be three because of the special meeting of the spirit. We were also shown how willing some people are to learn and too empty out, so we were able to fill up your vessels.

Blessings and joy from us all. TttA

WE MEET AGAIN!

Do try to take more time out and try to realize that you are still very much human, with very human feelings. Throwaway fear, doubt and worry, as only negative conditions come from these emotions, stay positive and don't dwell on yesterday's confusion. Let go of confused and fear based people, as they have to sort themselves out and don't transfer or 'take on' their old, historical fear based conditions. You need to stop and detach from them straight away as you don't need that kind of garbage. Look for something very positive to do or to say to someone today, you will carry out your work on the spirit stage. Little by little you will concur with them in the name of the universal light and again we say "go back and turn off the monkey chatter", we say "switch it off, let go and let God". It's simple but very effective so carry on doing your spirit work one day at a time and it will get you there. Remember that we are always with you so spend time talking to us, relaxing and smiling a little more, keep on taking what you do for now.

Lot's of love from your everlasting team. TttA

CALM AND JOY!

Let calm and joy be a big part of your day and it will help you to relax and prepare for tomorrow's work, don't look too far ahead, just one day at a time. Learn to completely surrender, and leave your spirit work, mind and body to us. I know that you have had tribulations for years, but some could have been avoided if surrendering had taken place earlier but we know it's hard for you to let go of old habits. Many will agree with you and understand what you are talking about though, sometimes the mind can be so pushy and won't want to take second place, still we say it's important to have your priorities in good order. We have promised to get you there so trust us and stay with that thought, keep special thoughts for special tasks. The same applies for medicinal substances; you must check how much of what and when to stop for a while. Your body has suffered trauma and will need extra certain things until it settles down again, so gradual progress is best for your body.

All our support and love. TttA

SUNSHINE AND ROSES!

Do remember to write, that way you will have the strength and wisdom to listen, believe in yourself more and miracles will unfold. In the last few days you have come to a new understanding of the eternal pattern, so much has been going on! There has been a new sorting of things, a new learning and a new way of looking at all the spiritual laws and how much you need to cooperate and connect. Still we say, "stay very close to the source", for as much as you evolve, you will experience physical symptoms in areas of weaknesses. One day you will be completely balanced and do more work for the light, little by little the fort will grow stronger and become more flexible. Don't try to see too much of the future, that's not for you to do, your trust and faith is improving so keep on working along that line. Your group will also increase so stay patient and let it all unfold. Your friend will sell and start a new life. Life is still unfolding and getting sorted so we send blessings for her work.

Lot's of love. TttA

LOVE AND LIGHT TO ALL!

Yes my children, there is so much more going on at the present time. You are so bombarded with negativity at present and to counteract that you need more from the light and us, you know it's true, so stay close and let there be light! No one on Earth really knows the full picture yet, so remember that you don't have to either, only that you should follow through with what we suggest, to be able to teach, advise and offer input is the way to present the positive side.

Cheer up all that enter your home, at times you wonder what purpose they have but that's not for you to know. Things will work out in the long run so don't spend too much time on those that do not listen, ignore and dispatch them and the air will clear. People and weather go together in swings and changes so make it your goal to balance your day and what's in it. Take all things with a grain of salt, that's the way it should be. The sun is always there, only hiding at times and when it is, do your work inside instead, but remember, only take one day at a time.

Love and cheers. TttA

FREEDOM AT LAST!

Remember what freedom means. With freedom comes responsibility and that's what choices are all about. You might think that to be able to make the right choice, at the right time is an everlasting quest but that's not so. You are getting there but stay patient and wait, we are looking after you and of late you have understood more. You had proof of that today when you experienced a miracle again, praise be for that. We are studying you down to the very core of your being and we know it's tough at times but you are getting there, your physical body is being looked after and what happened was only a reaction to your transformation. Your system needed an update so you are getting one, but beware of negative thought patterns, they have done you in in the past. Also beware of friends that think they know it all, they are not in control and they don't know it all. Send them love and light in big measures and surround yourself with a clear light bubble and all will indeed be well.

Lot's of love and light, together with a victory. TttA

SUNRISE!

A new dawn has come up over the horizon! You asked for this many times and before now we could not tell you as an increase in your faith and trust had to be activated before we could inform you and the other light workers of it. Stay close to the positive souls and let go of yesterday and yesteryears, you have had enough of that lesson and it's now time to leave and go forward. It will be hard at times but to be able to replace that situation with positive happenings and thoughts is far more beneficial for all those concerned. Bless each person that you come across and send love and light to all of them in a way that they will feel it and know where it has come from. We know that you are trying your best, just don't be disappointed when you don't see the results straight away, pace yourself. All things have there own timing, next Wednesday will be more inspirational. At present people are confused so be patient, calm, harmonious and joyful, this will help your physical situation.

Love light and cheer to you all. TttA

LET GO ONCE MORE!

Understand that letting go of one situation doesn't mean that nothing else will come along, take one situation at a time and don't get them mixed up. So much is hanging on how calm you can be and you need to remember to surrender and to mean it, monkey chatter and even a monkey mind will do nothing for you or anyone else. The spirit must to be in charge but the mind is often stronger and consequently you have many inquiries and thoughts that aren't positive, you still have a hard time staying clear of worries. It's an old pattern that's of no use any longer so try to remember to 'cut off' after dealing with work and surround yourself with bright colours, people and joyful thoughts. Take time out when you are feeling drained and tense, practical work will also enhance your life and sunshine will also help. You have asked for balance and harmony so embrace it when it comes. Transition time is hard on the system but fresh air and a fresh attitude will empower you, just stay steady and enjoy the moment. You will come through the transformation one day at a time.

Cheers and healing to you all. TttA

GOOD AFTERNOON!

Well once again you have lost some time, but we are aware that your personal timing has altered quite a lot lately. Last week you passed through another storm, a big clearance was done but your physical body was disturbed, it's only temporary though as your cell structure is being altered a lot, but it's so you can function perfectly again. The weather has also altered and it will continue to alter until you have just one season, which will be a very pleasant one, study nature and the animals to see what's going on. Last night you visited your two fathers, it was very important that you talked and even though it was only a beginning, it was something that you have wanted for a very long time. By talking with them they will get to know and learn from you and you will be able to settle things in your own mind. Questions of why, where and how will be answered and you can be assured there is a purpose to it all. Its purpose is one that you didn't know about beforehand because you had to come to a place of better spiritual likeness first. You needed to be able to understand the value of learning and to accept different ideals and beliefs, the path you walk on is very individual but it is leading to the same goal.

Lots of light, love and cheer. TttA

GREETINGS!

It has been two days since you last wrote. You will get it one day but first of all you need to understand that we are doing our part and that you need to do yours, the whole issue is one of co-operation and love. We understand that you still are in transition and that the whole of your life is being shuffled about. Eventually it will settle down but for now, as you know, you need to take things slowly at first. The vision of a light bright future lies ahead for you, so don't for a moment think anything else, so many situations were sorted, sifted and clarified last week. Today is also going to be a day of order and organizing, and while others still do not understand, for you it will make sense, ask us before hand to help out and we will be the bridge. Every dimension of work has it's own level, so ask again. Let go of the last of the old patterns, you don't need them or want them anymore and we also want to reassure you that you are fine and very much cared for, healing is given in full measure. This week will tell a new story, keep going and it will unfold, all is well and will stay well.

All our love and wisdom. TttA

ONCE AGAIN WE SAY FOCUS!

Do remember to set time aside, as before, it's hard at the present time but it needs to be regular, we have noted your determination to go ahead and leave past situations and conditions behind. A long time ago you got into a habit that allowed your mental brain pattern to be in control, that's not so anymore, now your spirit is in charge and it will stay that way. All the old patterns of negative thinking and disturbing ideas only caused you trouble and pain but now you can see the red thread clearer. It's been a hard lesson but you now know and understand how it's working, however you still have to be vigilant and positive to be able to go ahead, so don't think about tomorrow, think only of today. As of old, one brick at a time will build the fort. Support and encourage each other to stay strong, balanced and joyful, beware of negativity that tries to enter when least expected, just ignore it and smile.

Lot's of love from your loving teacher. TttA

GOOD MORNING!

Yes indeed it is! So much is cleaned and understood throughout the night and you don't always remember what goes on, but in time you will, for your information it's only work for the light. Genuine lightworkers committed to the light will be given more truth. You must be responsible for what information you give out, and you must prepare for your next encounter, at times you do wonder when and how, but don't, just follow through day by day. A faithful servant is a gem to us, we rely on your input and that is what we know you can do, so keep on doing as you are for now, a change of scenery would benefit you though. Remember to not get ruffled, no matter what might come across your path, it's all in hand, remember we only give you practical lessons. Let the day unfold, steady as she goes as we say, and remember to look at your guiding star. When stormy times and windy situations arise ask us to put soothing oil on the stormy waters. All is in hand and we do love you.

Care and protection from all of us. TttA

EASY DOES IT!

Let there be joy and relaxation in your life. Too much of anything is not good so try a little harder to find things to unwind with; colour and music is good but try to be a little more spontaneous. We know that you are going a little 'flat' but it won't last, the temporary situations are being sorted out and you will get rid of the other conditions. Carry on as usual and the time will soon go, don't concern yourself about tomorrow, the 'here and now' is more important than you think, look for little bright thoughts and actions. The long journey has made you a little weary but things will ease up soon, rely on companions and send out lots of love and light, some will not understand you at first, so everything has been put on hold for now. Despair is not your thing anymore, there will be a surprise around the corner, wait and don't make too many statements too soon.

Lot's of love in full measure from us all. TttA

LOVE AND LIGHT!

Once again you have tried hard to catch up, it has taken a while but so long as you try we will give you all the support that you need. Yesterday's event went well thanks to the fair one, she heard your call and responded; that's what we mean when we talk about cooperation and being relaxed enough to hear. Obedience to the teachers' guides and masters is most important, staying steadfast is another lesson, so even when you don't hear anything wait and ask again, then you can leave it to us. Doing otherwise will mean too much energy will go away and you need all you can get at present for your preparation work, which is now being activated. You will find that you will grow more than you dreamt you could, you need to believe miracles still happen even if so many have forgotten what they are all about, so stay calm, joyful and detached from all negativity. Rely on support, wisdom and a good architect; you know how that is so very important.

Enjoy and keep warm. Lot's of love. TttA

SUNNY WARM GREETINGS!

You now understand more, so we can start to go deeper together. You have started to see how things are unfolding and you need to keep those things in mind when you ask for wisdom. Remember though, that as you give out more wisdom and love, more, in good measure, will be re-entering your heart; that in turn will activate many other warm feelings from a long time ago, little by little the 'unfolding' time is arriving. You have asked about it quite often but for now you need to stay patient and keep going as you are, the big shift is coming closer. We cannot tell you when as yet, because so much depends on other combinations and events, but don' t concern yourself too much about the earthly timing of it, time is speeding up and at other times slowing down, so it's nearly impossible to tell. Surrender, let go and let GOD. We have heard your prayers and queries and they are important. They are also understandable, there is confusion and a lot of disturbance in the air, so stay clear and calm.

Loving thoughts from us all. TttA

A LITTLE MORE LIGHT!

A little more light will bring out the shadows, so they can be identified and understood by the divine light but take care not to over-do or under-do it though, as balance is one of the most important things in your life at this time. Too much energy is lost when you insist on not following through or following our wisdom. Unimportant pockets of distraction and disturbance will rear their ugly heads to test you, so stay alert and smile when they appear to you. You don't have to concern yourself about uninvited visitors or unwelcome conditions - we have all that in hand, you are becoming detached from all of that and consequently you're not so uneasy anymore. Your life is about to take a turn for the better, there will be more calmness, it will be easier to take one day at a time and other people will begin to understand who you are. You will experience a new look on life, one that is at ease but don't tell anyone if we say not too, wait until they ask you, then you ask us. To be a bridge in between is a responsible task, you have been trained and are now quite alert, and because you have practiced for many years you can understand others much better. Keep going and next week you will connect even closer still to the source.

Sunny and loving thoughts. TttA

OPEN YOUR DOOR!

That's a very welcoming idea, so many times you have come across shut doors and unfortunately it was meant to be that way at the time but by having a warm welcoming atmosphere you will be able to 'pull down' so many more barriers. It's all to do with removing stones that otherwise would take a long time to work your way around. As your group advances you will notice easier ways to connect with us. You'll be able to show others the ways of discipline and give them the will to follow through. Some will advance faster than other's but that has nothing to do with the quality of your work - it's because people are individuals. You must keep that in mind when you deal with someone on a personal basis. Enjoy your own. By the way another milestone has been reached. Also remember that as you advance, you will see how much more there is to learn and fully accept. Feel the warmth of our sun and its healing life force seep into your body. Enjoy friendly people, little bright happenings and don't overlook connections that seem unimportant, they're there for a purpose, all in all, the picture is forming.

Love and light to all. TttA

KEEP ON SETTING TIME ASIDE FOR US!

Yes, once again you have made it, congratulations. Your winter season is here now, so that gives you an opportunity to study and to grow deeper and higher. The two 'growths' operate best when there is a big root system and it enables you to shoot upwards. Visualize the mighty oak, when the storm comes you will be unbreakable and keep on giving shelter and peace too many, it's the same with the little acorn, such a little piece of life that grows into such a big tree, the same principle applies to you. Start off small and with lots of faith, love, learning and understanding, and one day no one and nothing will shake you or try to sidetrack you again. Remember your books, paintings and groups will be needed for the searching souls. Remember also that you still have to withdraw occasionally. As you know, to operate in so many dimensions, often in a very short time is a skill that we have taught you for your work, and is not to be taken lightly. Respect for us and others is fine but you must also do the same for yourself. It's not really a skill, more a recognition of the spirit. Lot's of loving thoughts from us all.

Keep on smiling. TttA

SUNSHINE AND LIFE FORCE!

My children of the light, this is what you must feed on too stay healthy, wise and joyful. Don't let anything or anyone stop that inflow of life. Go ahead, bath unhindered and unimpeded in the sunshine. Allow the life force to flow into you and you will learn so much more; don't ever stop learning and evolving. Stagnation is not for you or your many other light workers but it has certainly become an excuse for so many others. Thinking that you can only reach a certain plateau and that you will never see the view from the top will not enhance your life. You must always strive to go higher even if you are tired or weary. Don't

worry about what others think or see and don't wonder
when or how you can do it. Resting on a plateau is fine
but then you must go on with fresh new energy. We are
guiding you and last night we talked with you again, it was
powerful and very loving, your group work is unfolding
together with you. The road has been windy and winding
but it made you stronger and more understanding. Some of
your Lightworkers also have had that experience so they
know what it means.

Joy and blessings for you and your work and remember
the times from long ago. TttA

RAYS AND RAINBOWS!

Let my rays and my rainbows come in to your life and
home to cherish you. So much is going on and so many
people are involved so be patient and take one day at a time
and all will be well. Your friend B F is getting a lesson in
faith, patience and trust. She will be empowered by that,
feel a lot more settled and her new environment will also
help her to see more of the big picture. Taking time out
and recharging is a very good thing at this time and very
wise. Her change will come when the moon is full and will
happen quite fast and be very satisfactory for all concerned,
that you can rely on. The big surrender is very valid for
all that are working for the advancement for the change
of the Earth, so support and encourage each other with

love and consideration and we will do all we can to make the transition as easy as possible. Ask and smile more, we know how long a time it has taken and it's been a big challenge for many.

Eternal love and wisdom. TttA

LET GO AND LET GOD!

That's the best thing anyone can do. There is so much that you don't know or understand yet, but in time you will, as will many of your companions. You will stand united and be able to perform miracles as I did when on Earth. It's all to do with knowing about the universal and spiritual laws and all things are possible when you believe. You know that guidelines will always be given but when you are weary you have little frets and doubts. You have the ability to see when these situations arise, so surrender and let us deal with the whole situation, soon you will have new tools given to you. They are actually really old ones that you used to operate with a long time ago, but you will remember them and then you will work, with our guidance, much faster and with far less effort. Time is involved so wait and watch, they are likely to appear in the front of your very eyes.

Lot's of loving support from the ones that support and teach you. TttA

GODS GRACE!

Yes my dear, grace has come your way and you must remember that no matter what comes your way, we will always be there to guide and help you. Don't despair, even if you feel like it, as so much cleaning and 'letting go of' is going on, soon patience and balance will be yours. You are nearly at the end of your transition so hold on and you will conquer. Your physical body is showing signs of release and that means it will soon be cleared, we know this is so but you must trust in us until the very end of your lesson. Breathing exercises would be beneficial to you as this will allow calm and ease to return. We are sure that you will come through everything with flying colours so rest and recharge in between, look after your needs and trust your team fully. Carry on as usual and don't try to solve tomorrow's problems, leave them to us and be aware of negative thoughts. The holy war is still going on so don't get involved to deeply, as joy and harmony will still come.

What you have now is residue from the past and it will eventually go. TttA

GREETINGS CHILDREN OF LIGHT!

Enjoy today's little happenings and tonight we will be with you once again. Ask and you will receive, but be very specific about what you need. We know, but you have to learn that if you don't ask for what's best for your higher self, you will never receive. Also what you are asking for may not be what you should have, so practice, and keep on practicing and you will get there; to have a goal at this time is very valuable as wintertime is merely a time for recharging and an opportunity to go deeper. It would also benefit you to have a clean up in areas that have been forgotten for a long time. Your spiritual, mental and emotional needs need to be look at and if and when you surrender, DO IT. The fact that it is hard to let go at times is understandable but it would not be a positive thing for you to do otherwise. You know better than most how hard it is to let go of uncompleted situations because of what you have learnt from other similar past lessons. Nature is changing and so are you, so look to nature and learn, the patterns are the same and the seasons are a part of the pattern. It will all come together, but don't put a date on it as so much is changing and alterations are being made all the time.

Love and light as always. TttA

LET GO AND LET LIFE!

Yes that is so. To let go completely is the hardest thing for most and we have watched and taken notice of how hard it can be for you. At times it is easy because circumstances alter all the time, and as things are forever changing, so are you ever evolving. It's all about progress. Its like a little stream that has other streams flowing into it, eventually turning into a river, that then finally flows into and joins the ocean. It's a picture that you can easily remember and you need to apply it to your daily life. Later you can look back at how the unification had a very big part to play, it's all about working in a pattern and it's quite logical really. The universe is organized in such a way that all parts and levels flow as smoothly as possible. Remember 'order'; it's a word from so long ago but you can use it as a key, to remind yourself to keep your life in some sort of order, otherwise too many mixed energies will enter. Now it's time to deal with the next chapter. It will need our input to do it in a safe way, as diplomacy will be called for, so we will stay close in the mean time.

Courage and lot's of light and love from us all. TttA

GREETINGS!

Let's sit and talk for a while by the well of life, to rethink, recharge and restore. It has been a battle and a storm once again, but you did not break. It's what we mean by being flexible, go with the flow, don't over-do or under-do things. As we all know, you work best when you are in balance and harmonious. To be extra sensitive is fine, but use an extra buffer zone for it to be perfect, let us always guide you and lead the way. All the signposts do not do any good if they are not followed and when you are tired and unfocused, stop and pause for a while, clear your head and do your deep breathing. Yesterday was a beneficial day, a spiritual talk at the end of the day helped all concerned. The cleaning you have started is fine but only do a little at a time, writing the letter was a healing thing for your spirit, mind and body. Order is coming back to you so take that as a plus. Relax today, we will be around you and your physical grief will soon go.

Lots of love and wisdom. TttA

REST IN MY LOVE!

Remember to rest when weary and to change your scenery at times. Too much of anything will lead to weariness and a decreased desire to do anything else, so try to let life interest you and look at what is going on out there, but be aware of lasting impressions and how they fit into the picture. Much of what you leave behind might change people's opinion about you and your work and that's fine, but leave them alone if they are not coming to you. If they are hurried along, it will only cause obstacles of one kind or an other. Timing is really important, so waiting at times, is crucial, yesterday's event was just more proof of the importance of timing. You will see that the lady will recover better in another place, still, stand by and only act on our advice. Don't think about anyone ordering you to work, once again you will receive clear explanations and guide lines. We know how much work is involved for you to let go and to get rid of old grief and it's interesting to see the effect it has had on your emotions and your body. Not everyone has as strong a reaction as you do but the principle is the same. Cheers and hope from your teachers and friends.

We are standing by. TttA

ONE MORE BATTLE WON!

My Earthly children you have had such a battle of clearing, understanding and how to cope with negative and positive thoughts, but remember we will be with you tonight, and forever. It is a time when a lot of people will start to come out and start to believe and you will all have your part to play so stick to the plan. Individual paths and teaching will help and guide you. Lately there has been a lot of warring in the universe. This was what the Holy War was about as we have mentioned many times, so remember what we have told you before; "the Christ in me salutes the Christ in you". It will help, as you will know that you are a part of the God spark, meaning you are healing, learning and growing. For a long time you have been on your new path, and realignment has been taking place, you are being healed, loved, and gaining new teaching skills. Rejoice and remember you are a very powerful healer. Believe it deep down in your very soul. Glory to God. It's Thanksgiving time.

Love and light to all. TttA

GOOD AFTERNOON!

Well, the time has just passed by and so much has been done. With so many mixed up people and so much stirring, you have been given a lot of examples of how life operates, all so that you will never forget what's on the teaching chain. Today you have more patience and learnt how important it is to listen to us and now stabilizing is on the agenda, so stabilize. The old times when you used to go over the top are nearly over and that's so much better for you, so keep on believing and trusting. Ask and it will be given to you, let things run off you and send people up to us too deal with. Your human capabilities are not yet ready for the next level but keep working at it and remember that 'I AM' is more valuable than you think. All that is possible is being done for you to stay in tune and to teach you to accept help. Keep on restoring and working one day at a time and all will work out accordingly to the plan.

Lot's of warmth, wisdom and visions from us all. TttA

STAY CLOSE AND ON TIME!

Once more we say to you, "let go of distractions and outside disturbances". Enjoy the warming rays of my sun and the chance to be warmed by them in that unhindered and unimpeded way that we have spoken of before. It is necessary to clean up and kill off some undesirable factors and by allowing the sun and life force to do its work will give good results. Don't get down if certain people don't get the message or keep on coming back for more even if they are not listening. Many have been called to your group but very few at present are paying any attention to what's being passed on to them. Send blessings and light to them all and remember to send all these people to us, you will still be doing your part by being a bridge between the parties. Remember that no one is more important than the other and that there are different lessons for each different souls. Let all that's not good and helpful go, for good, otherwise it will drag you down and act as a ball and chain to your attitude. Cut all things that hold you to the past and remember to look ahead, and up. Peace and cheer to all that are helping out.

Keep in touch and all is well. TttA

GREETINGS!

Yes, once again you have got the idea right and we don't mind so much, as long as your intentions are right.

Remember we understand you and all of the different avenues of your life – so much is going on in so many different areas of your life and so much needs to be sorted out and understood for what it is. It will take time and you need to be patient. To grow is to evolve, so it's no wonder so many ask how and when it will happen. There are life times of lessons ahead for you and so many journeys, but you must never compare them with others. You need to just observe them so that you can start to understand better and consequently go ahead and be able to make miracles happen once again, believe and stay tuned. Life at present is so different and at times you wonder where you should be or how you fit in - leave all that for now, later on you will see and work with more conviction than ever. Child of the light, we are with you at all times and when you finally see us, it will make it so much easier. Smile and ask for help any time, day or night. Trust and talk to us, as you know you can.

Love and laughter. TttA

GOOD AFTERNOON!

Once again you have got sidetracked, you don't mean to, but life comes and goes. You need to understand that all things are changeable and that when things do change, you get out of order, so review your practical side and learn to relax and enjoy it, let go of 'ifs and buts'. Stay steady in your faith and know we are looking after your needs. Don't listen to others that don't give you respect, won't give you their time, or at the very least, accept your message and wisdom from us. They have a problem taking it all in, not reading you or only believing what they want to believe, but remember that has nothing to do with you. Drop them and send them to us with love and light. Go ahead with your other plans for today, lift your spirit and rejoice that you are doing your work and that there's more to come. Rest and all your medical situations will be restored.

Thank you and write again tomorrow, all is well. TttA

TRUST AND FAITH!

My children on Earth, you are having such a hard time understanding all the different changes at the present time. What's happening is that things are speeding up so that they can be finished before the big main shift, so keep on working and let the sun warm you and lighten your spirit. Don't think that you have not done all of your work. Why do you think nothing is happening? Much more is going on than we can tell you at this point and this is where faith comes into it, you have to learn that this is your path of study, learning and finally acceptance, it all comes down to learning about lifetimes of wisdom. Carry on and work as you are. Steady; the flame is burning and a lot of warmth, love and healing is coming from it so hold on to that thought for the remaining months, things will improve and you soon will be okay again. Let's remember that together. All in all things are on there way to completion.

Lot's of cheer, wisdom and love from us all. TttA

LET GO OF THE REST!

We are following your progress and we know how hard it is for you at times, but remember you are advancing and growing. We want to remind you that the hard times are only a temporary situation and you will only experience them while you are in transition. The transition will happen; it will occur but not overnight, as certain areas for you are very sensitive and so we are dealing with you accordingly. To be a whole unit is time consuming in some cases, but it is because of the conditions on Earth. That's a temporary thing also, but it will settle down and become a whole planet full of balance and beauty. It's a massive task to redo and change the conditions on Earth, but many teams are working it on it and the changes must be gradual so don't try to work to far ahead. You don't know all of it, only your part of the alteration, so stay patient and don't get carried away. Once again we are reminding you that this is one of your lessons so only do what's on your plate now, leave all other queries to us. Stay positive, leave us to carry out our work, keep your spirit up and smile more. It's good medicine.

Love eternal. TttA

CARRY ON ON YOUR WAY TO THE GOAL!

Steady as she goes, stay balanced and calm and you will get there. At this time of the year when not enough sun is showing you will need to replace heat in the best way you know. Take care with moist air, and drink plenty of water, movement will also help you along the way and before you know it you will see more of our sun and be able to enjoy life more fully again. It all comes back to the word balance so work and play, and when you do play, do what uplifts your spirit. Music and vibration are a couple of things that will enhance your life so try to use them. All in all you should nurture yourself, and others if they need it, but don't overdo any one part of your life. Keep on sending out love and light but also give to yourself, so that you can begin to recognize your own value and accept feedback when it comes. It's all right to look after yourself otherwise you will not be able to do your work to the fullest. Keep on saying "I am, I can, I will, I believe". It's a great help when you need to change thought patterns from the past.

Keep on keeping on, you will get to your goal sooner than you think. TttA

SUNNY RAYS INTO YOUR VERY SOUL!

Go out into the sun today and let the warm strengthening rays soak into your unhindered body and soul. Its colour is still the most important tool for your whole body, so stop, go out and feel that which is right for you today. It's an important part of your discipline and most times you are keeping it up, but don't 'skip' doing it because it doesn't seem important or because you are deterred by your human image. The calmness and healing it will give your whole body will benefit your whole being, so follow through with it. Your body is the vehicle for the temple of light and things will seem better when you relax in the sunny rays, just keep on telling yourself that all is well, and don't be concerned about things that don't really matter. Know that 'I AM'. We have told you that your concerns are for us to deal with, so by all means do your part and then hand it back to us to finish off, it's all a part of the work chain, don't do someone else's homework. Yesterday was a test and you did not get involved in the tangle, well done. Today you will have an experience in areas that occurred many eons ago, it will go very well and it will help you to transmit what we give you. Remember that we are always with you.

Cheers and health. TttA

RING YOUR BELLS!

Do try again. The sound of the bells of so long ago will help you to clear your mind and make you feel good but also keep playing your music, the vibrations of it will serve as an activator to higher levels, like a bridge between the two spheres. There are other symbols from other dimensions and a little at a time we will let you know what they are. For the moment, love and light will act as the road signals for you, to allow you to see through the veils and hidden entrances and to be able to reach all those imprisoned or tied down to one thing or another. You need to break down barriers and will have to put 'oil on troubled waters', but that is okay as so much is getting cleared out and because so many don't understand what's going on. You don't have to follow through with all of what we give you each day, but try too. As you well know, it's about keeping to a pattern. Beware of sitting and thinking too much, keep occupied and try to do cheerful things and have bright thoughts throughout the day. All is coming together at last, after a whole year of fine tuning and clearing.

Love. TttA

EVERLASTING LIFE!

You are able to see and hear more now, the picture is becoming clearer and after yesterday there is now a lot more light streaming into your heart and home. You can also see more of where you are going as much has been cleared away. Many will not like that, because they can't take anything from you, that you aren't giving freely to them anymore. That's okay, they need to do their own homework and clean out their own closets. Leave them to us, new people will come in and enjoy being with you and really listen to the truth from the universal knowledge source. Get organized and start to make room for new projects, they will be activated fairly soon. Look to nature, how it has its seasons and how it is being renewed after a time of rest. The lessons we give you to complete will be filled with practical examples like this. It's nearly been a year since letting go. It has been a hard time for you but it was necessary to allow you to go deep inside yourself so that it could all be looked at and sorted out. Drop the ones that are not respecting and honouring you.

Love and courage. TttA

LET MORE LIGHT IN!

Yes, the more light you let in, the less room there is for shadows. Ponder on that truth for a while. It's the same as looking after your garden – the more plants and colour you have, the less room there is for weeds. Sure, they're still there, but only to remind you of this truth and so it is the same with life. May goodness and mercy follow you throughout the day. The sun is now a little higher once again and you will benefit more this year than in previous years. Warm hearts and spirits will make it easier for you to survive the remaining winter month, so go out in your mind or whatever way you go out and give love and light from us. Again we say stay flexible, don't let small changes disturb you and try to catch up on your preparations. We have been, and are still looking at your actions and the times you struggle. We know what you have been dealing with but it is making you a stronger light worker. That it was not easy, is true, but it has helped you to understand so much more, it's all to do with getting back to the school of life.

Pink light and blue healing from your team. TttA

ONE DAY AT THE TIME!

Yes my friend that still stands. It's too easy to get mixed up in the tangled webs of some people, so stand by, but don't get too close. Yesterday you had more proof of a spirit connection and how you can use positive mind power to activate situations, focus and to move along, it's great when it's called for but don't overuse it. It's about keeping a balance in all areas and that's one of your lessons, to know exactly when to stop, if you need too, ask for a sign and we will deal with that. The warmth of the sun has once again lifted your spirit, and tonight you will receive extra terrestrial healing and information, but try to remember that the more you let go and surrender, the more you will benefit from our input. Still, a few minor changes will be shown to you and once you see them you will know why. Alterations for the better will also come in all four areas. Stay in tune, we are behind your work and we know how it is for you, the unknown is not for you to be concerned over, that's our task. Try to drink more water.

Lot's of lovable thoughts. TttA

SORT OUT TIME!

Now is the time to let go and to welcome the new, it will be okay but it needs to be done at night. Try to remember to not get involved in other peoples situations, things will come right in their own time but the people involved have to learn to do their own work, because as you know, no one advances that does not put the work in. Accept the situation as it is and then sort out for yourself what to keep and what to let go of. The whole picture will become so much clearer when the main picture has been looked at. After it has all settled down, you will be able to add on what you need and have a more useful life. We understand that it's not easy for many but it would be wise. Today, you have once again seen situations that could have been avoided and that would have been, in more ways than one, less costly. They were valuable lessons and even though there were a lot of other distortions happening at the same time, you understood

214

what was going on. Remember that you will never get a clear picture and that it is also very energy draining. Rest for now and start afresh tomorrow, you have time to learn from life and some afternoon sunshine will put rays of light on everything.

Love and wisdom. TttA

SPIRIT SECURITY!

Yes my Earthly children, security under my umbrella is a promise, feel guarded and safe for you are indeed protected. Distractions to your spiritual and emotional needs can be quite severe at times, so don't let other thought forms slip in and disrupt your progress. Try to remember we are with you and always will be. Your daily journal is a good inspiration for the many different souls at different times, it works for everyone as and when they need help, but you need to keep doing it, as only we know the whole picture. We will help you to write it because only we know what is needed for each soul. Stay sensitive to colour and situations around you, they are there for a purpose and to be learnt from. Remember, they are a powerful source of help and a rich source of wise material that will enable you to use the best possible cures, so stand back and look up for a sign that will enable you to see what's going on. Keep on sending out thoughts of love and light to those entering your sanctuary and to the ones that you are keeping in your thoughts and spirit.

Love eternal. TttA

KEEP ON LIGHTING A LIGHT!

It all helps on those grey days, the light and the incense will bring your soul up to a higher level and it's also a reminder about life itself. Always counteract the shadows and the not so happy thought patterns with love, music and joy. Keep warm and stay close to us to gather the strength to keep going towards the light. The energy and clarity of it is about to change to show you new ways. Sensitive people will have to work harder to stay detached from negative thoughts, actions and the self appointed people who know it all. You will succeed and go ahead on your path but keep vigilant and let us do the rest. If you don't and count upon your own knowledge without knowing all the facts, you will go wrong. Wait for us, to be careful and to listen in is very wise. We want to keep reminding you of some of the old knowledge; that it is good to occasionally look at it again, it's like a turnover and reactivates energy. Have a break and let go of the rest. We are still standing by.

Lot's of love from us all. TttA

FRESH START!

Once again you are experiencing a fresh start. All the old patterns are mostly worn out and are of no use to you anymore because you have developed better thought and energy patterns and better timesaving practices. Expect miracles, you have already had quite a few and they are to let you know we are very much alive. At times you have been surprised at how fast solutions have come to many of those that are close to you, so keep watching, looking and seeing what's going on. To stand back from the situation will also help a lot, you are dealing with many situations at the same time, so you need to separate them, it's a part of your learning, to help you with discipline. Remember to focus on today, yesterday is gone. Be thankful that you are able to do as much as you are doing but try to unwind in between a little more. Your body will appreciate it and act accordingly. Today's sun will recharge you, give you more life force and top up your energy levels so take advantage of it and use it to change little things in your environment especially things that feel stale. Our blessings upon you and your work, we have noticed the change in you, keep on keeping on.

Amen to that. TttA

GO AHEAD AS PLANNED!

To do just that will be fine, still, only take one day at a time and it will soon pass in to a new order. The sun will shine on you and show you the way, it will be a light on your path that shows you the road signs. It's been carefully drawn up for you like this and it will be given to you a little at a time, but beware of fears, unease and falsehoods, once in a while they will come up, to check how you handle them and how well you are learning from them. Your control of the present situation is taking a little time, but when it's all done you will be completely restored, it might feel uncomfortable for now but don't spend too much time on it, the money side will also be taken care of. Tonight there will be another initiation and it will benefit all concerned; they will understand more. My miracle healing powers will come upon you today and ease the situation, rest, do more of your deep breathing exercises and please be assured that all is well.

Love. TttA

FAITH AND MORE FAITH!

That is what will get you through one day at a time, but take it slowly. The sun is shining today again, so take it as a sign of goodwill and enjoy the warmth. We are with you at all times so don't worry too much. One of the reasons we are here for is to remind you of what you already know, and have known, for a long time. Just remember to follow through on our advice, no one is stronger than God and miracles still happen, so believe and it will happen. I am, I can, I will, I believe, NOW. Understand that these words are intrinsic to universal law in action. There's so much you don't understand yet, but you are learning, it will take time but you are a very good student, just remember that you are heading towards healing and completion. You have a few friends that want only the best for you and consequently you can rely on them fully. Go ahead today and enjoy the peace we are sending you, together with healing and reassurance.

Love and light from us all. TttA

BLESSINGS BE UPON YOU.

My children, today we shower blessings upon My Earthly children. Many of you are working very hard to get through and at times you feel you are making no progress, that's not so, you are only waiting, pausing for a while and that's fine. To take time out is very beneficial. Let go of some problems if we say so, in some cases you don't always know what's best so therefore you would be better off to surrender and get a higher power to deal with it. The results will be faster and better and consequently you will move further along your path and be able to guide others that are still in the dark, but remember to rest in between. Your path in this lifetime is a strange one; there is so much to clear up and so much to let go of, it's a mammoth task of sorting, understanding and revealing things. At times you think it is all too much, but it is unfolding, in it's own time. Keep up your faith and trust and send love to all, including yourself. Tell yourself that deep down in your heart all is well and it all will be kept up to date with your healing and support. Remember also that you can claim miracles, so Amen to that. Hope and clarity to the little one.

Love light and laughter. TttA

EVERLASTING LIFE!

To be able to see even a glint of eternity is really a gift and as you spend more time with us and renew your strength, we will give it to you. When you understand more we can give you even deeper truths. Don't feel that you have to try and do more each day, only do what's on your plate at the time, you will know when and how soon. Get through one day at a time and don't look too far ahead, you will get there eventually, and healing, wisdom and supplies will be given to you, as you need it. Yesterday you made progress with your Father; it's been a long time since you had a talk that deep and the more you connect with him, the better it will be, so keep the contact going. Get to know him all over again, he does not yet understand you, but in time he will. Also so many others that have gone before you will connect. The day will come when you will see again and then you will recognize many. The support and healing is there, so take it. Open up to more trust and peace and let it enter your heart so you can help and support others. Believe and trust and it will all become yours to cheer and enjoy.

Love and light. TttA

REJOICE!

Do just that. Wonders are unfolding and just because you don't see them as yet, they are still happening, miracles are also on the agenda. All is in the melting pot and you will be very surprised when you see the results of it all. Well, it's been a hard time for a very long period but it was necessary for your growth and understanding, take heed and go ahead but remember not to push ahead too fast. 'One thing at a time' as the saying goes and when you feel ready, look again to see if it's the right thing to do. Beware of people that try to push ideas on to you, or try to give you advise without being asked for it, that's not respect for your spirit. The same applies to you when you see a 'condition', wait if we don't say anything at first and then say what you have to say, but always after asking us first. So many only ask about the ego, and forget that the spirit is in charge. Human conditions are all so different so you need to learn how to think higher and wiser.

Love wisdom and health eternal. TttA

YESTERDAY IS GONE!

Yes it is so, so leave the days that have gone behind and don't think about them any more, time will heal and help you. Do more breathing exercises and remember that the 'deep holds' need to be done without interference. As you will come to understand later on, there is a lot on the agenda and things could easily get mixed up otherwise. Also remember that sensitivity is fine when you are doing your work, just not when you are in public or when your mind is 'playing tricks' on you and causing you to have doubts about what to do next. When that happens withdraw and clear your mind; something done in haste will never turn out right. Only when the spirit prompts you, is it okay to act fast. When you are weary rest for a while and renew your strength, otherwise the stress will only cause you to lose energy and at present you need as much energy as possible. Allow also, the sunshine to enhance your life and the lives of many others. Don't try so hard to unfold your life, it will not work that way, we have your life in our hands, so let us. We are sorting out the future for you and your emotional, mental and spiritual needs will be taken care of, the whole picture will be balanced.

Love and healing for you and yours. TttA

COURAGE!

Yes my child of light, you have been tried and tested so many times and sometimes that's too much for some, but not for you. It's all to do with your future work here on Earth, so keep going and don't look too far ahead. You are getting there but do try to relax a little more between jobs. This morning you had another student sitting at your feet once again, you knew her in another lifetime in Holland. She does not know it yet, but she will appreciate it when she accepts it; slowly but surely it will come together and it will be one more piece of proof for you to strengthen your faith. We are still looking after you and your companions but it's a big circle of connections to connect with once again, some will learn fast and others will take a long time. Compassion comes from the star Vega, where the human race started and that's why you often go back there so you can feel at home and learn more.

Healing and light to all light workers. TttA

A BIG TURN AROUND OF EVENTS!

This is what will happen! We have noticed your work and progress and the many times you have practiced what we have taught you, sometimes several times in one day and soon there will be a turn around in events. It's to let you know that we are there for you and to protect you so keep on spending a little more time in meditation and doing your deep breathing, the sooner you learn to cut off from the world, the sooner you will receive the wisdom from us. It will tell you that there is a pattern to life and how universal law is working for the better, but beware of falsehoods and spirit lechers. Some will try and they will think they are succeeding but others will soon leave when they realize who you are and what you are talking about. Many of them have low spiritual understanding and only think about material things, it's not their spirit that is in charge, just their mind mostly. Practice watching how people's eyes react to you, the little child that you met yesterday knew straight away and it was good for you to see that. We are never far behind. Keep on going as you are and you will get there, let go of a few more articles, they will be useful for some. A new hobby would be good.

Clarity and recognition. TttA

RELAX AND ENJOY!

Take time out and enjoy life a little. Lots of little happenings and small-unexplained situations have been occurring lately, but they're just signs of the times and you just need to go along the best way you can and know that all is in hand. The women 'A' is not in charge at present; four entities are playing games with her and they have been trying to infiltrate you, it didn't work, but you had an unpleasant experience every time you got a glimpse of them but now that you know, you can handle her. We will deal with her. We'll clean her up, then seal her to stop others moving in on her and at last you will be free to do what you want. She will not know what happened to her, but you will, watch and see. Go on with other work today and be grateful that you got an answer at last, tomorrow is another day, so let things be today and start afresh tomorrow, it's wise to relax and smile. Easy does it and say thank you to the universe for the unfolding. Amen to that. Rest for the remaining time today.

All our love from the whole team. TttA.

NEW LIFE!

A new life involves letting go of the past but leaving room for life, health and wisdom in your new situation, so bless this day, breathe in the fresh air and fill your lungs with all that is fresh and valuable. The old 'no good' values have to go, but remember to keep what's good; the knowledge from the past will be of good use. Don't be so quick to judge, it's faster for sure, but at times it can lead to wisdom being lost and good advise being ignored; be selective but not too much, it all comes back to that old word balance, and to be able to see what's what. In your case you need to ask us first, and then go by your gut feeling. Also, at present you need to withdraw a little more, too many people and ideas can easily crowd out your day, and it's the same with your work and being able to take time out with others. That need is different for everyone so you must understand that the recharging is different for different people. Let the day unfold as best as it can and let there be no more doubt, fear or unease. You tend to pick up the fear, frets and pain from others and that has to stop this minute, don't compare yourself with others as they are not on your path. Have courage.

Lot's of love and peace. TttA

CALM IN THE STORM!

To be able to stay calm in the storm is indeed a gift. It will not come straight away; sometimes it takes years for some and yet others can be enlightened over night so don't compare, everyone's path is so individual. These are the lessons to be learned and the wisdom to be practiced again and again. At first you might not always see it but eventually the red thread will show up and then you can be sure it's all working for the best, for all concerned, every life affecting others. No one lives by and for him or herself, there are always others involved, so you must always check with us first, don't make rushed decisions.

At present there is so much going on so be patient, things are about to get sorted, but slowly does it – it gets so tangled at times. The activation of the photon belt is also on the agenda and that involves so much sorting and exposing so don't expect your little problem to get priority, when we think it's time it will be done. Our timing is so different to yours so stop trying to work it out, "go with the flow" as we have said so many times before. "Sit by a riverbank, watch the river flow and visualize where it goes; some braids go to the oceans, others to big rivers and it's the same with your work for the light; many small streams make a big river flow".

Love and life. TttA

ENJOY AND REJOICE!

Once again you have seen what prayer will do and because of it there has been many surprises, with many still to come. Small happenings and wonder will unfold, some even in your own life. When all the past feelings and hurts have been healed you can enjoy life and you will smile again. You are nearly there so hang in and let us do our work on you. We can understand your queries at times, they're natural, but the picture must unfold a little at a time to suit your sensitive system. Sometimes you wish you were not as sensitive as you are, but because you are, you pick up spirit messages faster and clearer. Now enjoy the warmth of the sun coming in to energize, soothe and heal you. Thank you for lighting a pink candle for us this morning. We are aware of your life and how it's unfolding. Also, the release last night was from the old days with your friend K, that's all right and her concern for you was valid and appreciated, and she will understand more in time so keep on sending her love and light. She is sensitive also but on a different level, your Father will mediate. Your other friend A is starting to clear her eyes.

Love and support. TttA

LOVE AND LIGHT TO ALL!

Once again you have got the message that the two most important factors for you to have are growth and light and that they feed the spiritual, mental, physical and emotional areas. Many times you have looked at other remedies and that was fine, but the simplest and easiest way is with love and light. That means real eternal love and light, not just some emotional word that Humans use for their different agendas. When you have experienced the real feelings of love and light, you will know straight away when something or someone is trying to fool you. Many think that you don't know or that you don't understand them fully, but they don't really know you, they only know what they think you represent. It's not their business to know, nor is it your business as to what you see, leave that to us, it will save you more hassles and energy. We are following up with the women A. She is still confused at times, but has started to think. You yourself have started letting go of some thought patterns and also given away what no longer serves your life best, that is good. The sun is also trying to reheat many sad and frozen hearts and therefore it is a time to speak up. Don't expect others to follow straight away, you are not on the same level as them so you will have to wait, but keep on working, a little bit at a time on what you are working on. Remember not to look too hard for an answer for the future of your life. It's in hand.

Trust and don't be afraid. TttA

SUNNY VIBRATIONS!

Do keep an eye of where you go, what you pick up on and if you're not sure about something let it be. When you return make sure you cleanse and also drink water. Metal and water are very strong conductors so make a mental note to remember that and follow through with your cleansing and drinking; clear guidelines and thinking will save you a lot of energy. Go forward unafraid and know that we are with you throughout your joy and tribulations. It all takes time, especially in your case as your system is so finely tuned. Because of your work you were given extra sensory perception, which is not always easy to live with, but you promised before you where born and now it's all happening. Now as you understand more it will give you more confidence to pass it on to others. No one gets a gift like that unless they pass it on to others, but follow our timing and don't move too fast, the circumstances may not be right just yet and therefore you may not achieve the best result possible. Your physical condition is only temporary so stay with us and all will be well, your spirit is soaring up to us faster than before. Courage, belief and healing from all the past happenings.

Glory to God - Amen to that. TttA

LET GO AND IT WILL FLOW!

This is just one more lesson that people do not fully understand and even with you it's a long-standing issue; to let go of everything is hard work so ask us for help. Peace and help will come to those that have the will to start a new life. You will be free from all the things that stop you from going ahead and from having to drag past lifetimes with you. Let it be so today, follow through and it will happen. Now is also the time to look at many emotional and spiritual thoughts. You have seen and heard so much this week, so it is time to uncover what is hindering the progress. Some uncomfortable physical conditions will appear, but that's temporary, stay alert and go with the flow as much as possible. They will pass, it's only the body reacting to fear, disappointment and 'hurts' from so many past lives and is usually no reason to seek a medical appointment, just allow your spirit, mind, body and emotions some rest. The spirit is in charge and will reign over the mind, but in saying that, your mind is still very good at the job it was meant for. Every part of you is programmed for certain types of work and if something happens to distort the pattern, things get out of order and the life of the person is distorted. Let God sort out what's going on and listen in in silence. May God bless you all.

Thank you. TttA

TOGETHER AGAIN!

You may wonder at times where we are because you don't always see us when you need reassurance, well that's understandable, you are still human, so for today let the sun warm your body all over and let our love make you feel loved. Early last night you met with others from the universal team and then later on you visited here. There was a lot of healing and loving that went out to you and afterwards you relaxed like never before, you soaked up all we gave to you. Now try to stay steady and as relaxed as you were then, it will help and enhance your whole being. Take one day at a time and trust, faith and love will get you into a new life. Believe in what we gave to you, even if it is only a little bit at a time. You are now free, but the 'long time coming' has made you tired. All that was trapped for so long from such a long time ago has left you changed but don't concern yourself with that. It may be gone – it may not be, but when we say it has, you won't need to ask again. Just because you don't have any guarantees doesn't mean that you will be left out or neglected, so keep happy thoughts in mind and a warm environment around you to allow you easier movement of your body. Let today be a calm, recharging day, perhaps there will be a visit from somebody or a cheering phone call.

Blessings and courage from all of us. TttA

ONCE AGAIN WE MEET!

So often you want to be on time but there is so much going on, so don't despair my little one. At present there are so many changes going on around you and the 'clearing up' is on going, so a few things will have to wait a little longer. Time will eventually get rid of the unwanted situations. The same goes for the weather – soon there will be sunshine, rain and stillness. If you look at your animals they will show you how much things are altering. Conditions at present are temporary, so don't spend too much time trying to solve the mysteries. We have it all in our capable hands, so let us organize the events. The sun is now returning; only one more month to go and then it will be the beginning of spring, which is always a time for clearing and cleansing. Last night proved that the practical details need to have an eye kept on them. It's too easy to forget things when you are tired or not focusing, all misgivings will work out well in the end. You are doing what you can so wait for instructions and in the mean time relax and take time out, tomorrow night will very good, most beneficial for all concerned just don't try to live in the future. There is enough time in each day when it comes. Many people have lessons to learn including you before the photon belts activate.

Blessings and rewards. TttA

THIS IS A NEW DAY!

Remember every day as you awaken, that it's a new day and the healing that is going on and the fresh start will make it easier for you to handle. By holding on to the past, you are dragging up past feelings and past experiences, but you mustn't think of them as a waste because they're for you to learn from.

You've been learning one lesson at a time and you're starting to get there, it's just that so much has happened in between so some things got held up. That's okay, but start afresh again. Your winter weather is hard on your physical body, but we are working on a new weather pattern, one that is better suited to your living style, still, we say "go easy on yourself". It's all about having a balance in all areas, the time will come soon enough, to go out and sit in your magical garden. Nature is the best healer and we do know how hard you are trying to get it all done. To relax and unwind is hard for you, but we are taking the time to be with you to speak with you about your life, your work and the conditions around you. You have to spread a little sunshine around and that means for yourself as well; it should always be equal, equal amounts for each situation, including time and that when you overdo anything, another part will always suffer. Maybe that's why you get so drained at times. Let go and let God take over. Trust, faith and love will make your life so much easier and more joyful, let us do the work, as you know we are.

Courage and health. TttA

ONWARDS AND UPWARDS!

Stay on track and keep on working, another hurdle has been climbed. The releasing time is here and you will soon realize that you only need to shift around a few items and the energy will change. It's hard at times to think afresh, but it's okay, the communication will be better and closer. Yesterday's meeting was very healing, you were all very connected to us, many healers were there with you and the introduction to the star people went fine. We received your love and light, thank you. The closer you all become the better and stronger you will all feel and operate, united is best at all times. The sorting out is still going on, so be patient and alert. Your health is going to be fine; your whole system is being redone and that's why so much unpleasantness has been happening and will continue to occur, but it's only temporary. Time will speed up or slow down depending on what is needed. The spirit in I and L is awakening very fast now and they will have the opportunities to practice what we have passed on through you and what they have been inspired to learn throughout their travels in this lifetime on Earth. It will also serve them well as they carry on in the next life, as they evolve, enabling them to help themselves and others.

Thank you for opening your heart and home, blessings be upon you My child of light. TttA

ALL IN IT'S OWN GOOD TIME!

When you awaken each day and ask for guidance, you often think it will happen; well, we made the law, so when action is needed, you will get an answer and if help is needed we will send you just that. Of late you have seen how organized we are and you would do well to listen. Your life is about to change and we will tell you about it in our own way but first, all connections have to be connected for it to work, leave all that to us. Today you experienced a lot of practical help and whatever was meant to be activated will have been. Your medical situation is also about to experience another miracle. Your whole body has been put through a mighty experience because of the work that will be required in the future, but don't ask about that just yet, it's not the right time. You are dealing with areas from such a long time ago but the unease and pain will only be temporary; you are dealing with it bravely and courageously. It's what you are and the transformation will benefit you and your work. Your spirit knows so give it a chance to spread the light.

Blessings and light from us all. TttA

GOOD TIDINGS!

It's always good to hear good news, to be able to cheer and uplift and to pass it on to others. Be positive and take one day at a time, time will soon pass and when spring comes it will enhance your whole life. Stay alert and leave your actions in our hands, I am your father and I am looking after you, little frets will not disturb you or your progress, you are handling it all with wisdom and grace. It has been a long time coming so be glad it's here, take notice of the little smiles, cheers and sparks that are here and there. We are staying in contact every day and every night but don't concern yourself with when or how, we have promised we would deliver, so believe our words. The big picture is becoming clearer so rest assured there is a solution around the corner that you haven't thought about. In the mean time carry on as usual, enjoy a little time outside and inside, a big change of energy is about to emerge.

Blessings, in the mean time for all. TttA

GO AHEAD UNAFRAID!

Courage, wisdom and a map will be given to you to show you the best way to deal with energy situations, this is why yesterday's phone call will be important in the future. Souls searching for the path have always been a part of your work here on Earth and you mustn't feel that because you act as a channel for healing that you don't have to do what we ask. You are only able to connect and work through us because you can act as a channel for healing and wisdom for the benefit of all mankind. You are placed where you are, because of this special work. In a month's time you will experience a new feeling and will look at life from a different angle. Today's work is to tie up loose ends and prepare for tomorrow night. More people will come to your circle, Some will come and stay only once, while others will come back regularly. Don't concern yourself with the once only visitors, some were only curious, while others were not ready. There will be a sorting out of who wants to spend time with the spirit learning how things should be. Still, we say don't look too far ahead, learn how to enjoy the moment, a little at a time is better than a whole lot at once. Spreading the joy and positive feelings and emotions in your case, will rebuild your confidence and make you feel strong once again. Let other people do as they decide, there's no point telling anyone, if they don't ask.

Rejoice and learn. TttA

BLESSINGS!

So much depends on our blessings and if and when we do make suggestions, you need to listen! You are getting better at doing just that, but when you are tired or stressed you forget. That's only human but try to improve on that pattern; you can and you will be able to if you try, believe and all will be well. Your friends are studying your life and they want to ask about certain aspects of it at times, some do now, but later on more will. Tomorrow's meeting will go well, the purpose of it all is not yet clear but we will let you know in plenty of time. The soul of B is getting restless, and want's to know where to start, you will do your part and similarly, others will fill in the gaps. He does not easily accept new truths, sometimes he will, but he also tries to alter things for his own benefit and that's not right. He knows that, so don't say too much, go on with your practice and don't worry, the learning experiences you are gaining are all you need for now. As you know, sometimes, just too much learning at any one time can only be confusing for you. The warmth from the sun is reviving for you, so go out and naturally bath in it in. Relax in your human body and dismiss any thought of shame or embarrassment, let it relax you, take it easy in the 'in between' times. There is a system to it all and we are very organized, it's just that human's that keep on changing their attitudes and actions. To be steady is best and in stormy times cast your anchor and wait.

Blessings in one hundred fold. TttA

FINALLY!

We know what's been going on but the main thing is that we haven't lost contact, just because you have not written does not mean that we haven't communicated. Many times we have met at night when you have relaxed and we have given you the healing and loving input that you need. So much is going on within the make up of you as a person. You have a new perspective on life and it is giving you the strength to follow through with what's needed. Every thing is in good working order now with only a little residue from the big change and a new order is about to emerge for you, so take one day at a time, and all will be well. At times you feel so tired, but it's only temporary, just keep occupied and relaxed. We are sending you healing every night, so know that your physical needs are being looked after. The weather is improving but it's still cold at night so make sure you stay warm and rested. Don't concern yourself about the future, no one can tell you what it will be at this point, just know that it's so different that no one actually knows, leave it to us and carry on as you are. Things will be dealt with in the most beneficial way for all concerned, what's meant to be, will be. The big picture is emerging so wait and watch for a new dawn.

Lot's of love, care, courage and growth. TttA

LET'S TALK FOR A WHILE!

It's good to communicate with each other. A good exchange of energy and the building of a good friendship is something that you all would do well to try to do more often, so, keep up your work and think positive conditions and outcomes, it's your choice so make it a good one. What's going on with you now is only the residue of all the cleaning up and as your system is so sensitive you suffer more severely. The warmth of your healing, the vibrations from others and the lighthouse are all working to benefit you, at times you can't see the results, but don't be concerned, leave it to us, your prayers will be answered and you will have your miracles. When others see what's happening to you, they will believe that it's possible for them. We are dealing with you every night and also with the women 'E. A.', at times she is confused, but she is trying. Keep believing and trusting as much as you can, but stay relaxed, you will get there. Because of your long line of past lives it's more involved than many others, there are many that think they know how to help and they mean well, but they haven't got the full picture. Listen to them and then sift. Go on with your day in our peace and remember we love you.

Courage, wisdom and light. TttA

PEACE TO YOU ALL!

Without peace nothing can be achieved. You have a hard time to find it in your heart sometimes but that is because of all the happenings around you. As we always have said many times before, detach and relax and when you do, everything will fall into place, in divine time. If we relax together it will happen. So much has been coming to the surface lately and with your system it can't be too much at once. Now that you are rebuilding a new life with hope, health and happiness you need to believe and trust that it will be so. Despair we can understand but it's only temporary, it will pass. Still, only take one day at a time, you are still in a transition, there's a while to go before it's all over and you can start to live once again. Carry out what we give you and don't think about tomorrow too much. Help is on its way, so stay strong and calm, you do have helpers and supporters but you need to let them know what you want and then wait for the results. Rest and recharge for the rest of the day. Blessings be upon you.

Love and light. TttA

STORMS MIGHT RAGE AND RAIN MIGHT FALL!

Let nothing put you off working with the spirit and staying close for good input. We know what you are experiencing and it might be harsh at times, but you need to get used to all kinds of conditions, it's only practice and with practice you become stronger and more resilient. Don't concern yourself with these earthly situations, but as long as you are working there keep an eye on what's going on. The animal and the plant kingdom also feel what they don't understand and their reaction is to sleep and all will be right, it's a basic survival technique for them. For humans, you need to rest, relax and recharge for busier times ahead. I hear you think, the sooner the better. Let your home act as a sanctuary for many. There is too much unease and restlessness everywhere, so try to spread as much joy and calm as possible to whom ever you connect with and tell them about the better times ahead. In the meantime do your daily inputting and never give up on hope, love and charity; keep calm and warm so that you can give extra, of what we give to you, to others. Our storehouse is so full that you only have to ask. You do just that, every day and that is good. Quite a few are still in denial about our teachings but leave them to us. We are beside you so rest assured that all is well. Trust, love and faith are still the three most important words.

Cheer and courage. TttA

PEACE AND JOY TO ALL!

Let our peace stay with you throughout the day and let it come in to your very soul. As the days unfold over the next while it will become clear to you that you are now working on your next progress, with a lot of positive input. A few days ago you had a revelation about how to deal with people, that was good. Now when you have said your piece, you can unwind and have your life back, in order again. There was so much, for such a long time that you needed to get through to people and when you thought you had been successful but hadn't been, you didn't stop, a different approach was all that was needed. Today you have started to unwind at last, so you can return to what you used to be. Today the warmth returned to your life force so tonight will be interesting. The aquamarine stone will help you to continue to heal and will give you visions. Remember though that you are still in a changing time but when the metaphysical changes are complete, you will settle down and feel more at ease so stay close to positive and calm people in the meantime, it's so easy to get side tracked now. Later it will become clearer as to where your path is leading you and for what purpose but for now it's the unfolding time, so unfold.

Blessings and love from your whole team. TttA

BELOVED!

You have to remember that you are cherished and loved by us all and by so many on the earthplane, but you mustn't have thoughts of despair or hopelessness. We are helping you and we are looking after your health in all areas, but you need to let us help you. You are getting so tired from trying to do too much on your own, so just ask us for help, as often as necessary and it will come. So, about your beliefs - you do believe, we know but at times you have doubts, because of circumstances and because you spend too much time alone, however you know what to do, you just want back up and to see us. It will happen. So many are visiting you at night and so many are supporting you, you only need to believe that you will see us and it will happen. Your physical conditions will be healed as well, this is not a big problem, we have promised to look after and heal you, so hold on to that thought. We are responsible and reliable so trust us and don't be afraid. Yesterday was a new beginning so today you can let go a little bit more, expect miracles and don't stop your spirit from blossoming. It's on its way.

Love and laughter from us all. TttA

KEEP GOING AHEAD!

Understand that to change from earthly conditions to a much higher sphere will involve a lot of changes

- spiritual, mental, emotional and physical changes. Be aware of them but don't be alarmed. Watch for changes and differing moods in yourself and the people that come to your door. Being aware of these things will allow you to see how people react to honest conversations and also to your body language. Also listen to the feelings you are experiencing from what you get from the media. Now is a time of awareness, alertness and anticipation, the waiting time is hard for many but it will be worth waiting for, so much is in the melting pot and so much is being uncovered. It's not really what you thought it would be at first, but as you look deeper in to it, you will be able to see what's going on. When you are to close to a situation, you can't always see clearly, so stand back and ask for the mist to clear, if you don't, you are likely to make the wrong decisions and that would hold you back and cost you a lot of energy and time. Please, stay close for a while, we will show you our concern, which way is best for you now and later you will be able to see us.

Lots of love and cheers. TttA

GRATITUDE

Remember to give thanks and be grateful for all the various actions, healing, wisdom and peace of mind you receive but also remember to give thanks to your teachers and healers, they like the communication and interaction.

My faithful servant of old and new thanks you also. It's a trial time at present, you are all being tried and tested but its for a purpose - to see how much faith and trust you all have in your heart. We have trained you now for many years and it's finally bearing fruit. It's taken a lot of practice, a lot of lessons and also meant repeating a lot of practical experiences for you to finally see what's going on but it has all helped and taught you that life is taking you on a journey towards your goal. Soon courage and joy will follow. It's not always going to be so slow and painful, you are now over the biggest part, so keep on having faith and trust in yourself and the source. We are rejoicing with you today so keep up your good work. We are noticing a change in your attitude, just stay alert and positive.

Love, my cherished one. TttA

OUR FATHER - THE CREATOR!

Yes my earthly children, I am, and you all should know how much you can depend on me to be just that. To depend, to surrender totally, in today's world is indeed a rare gift. The planet is in an uproar over all the changes and only so many take the chance. You would all do well to surrender to the Father that knows all, sees all and hears all. He has the complete picture and by doing so you will achieve the best possible outcomes. You humans are not yet able to see the blueprint, so acting without all the facts you will not make progress for anyone. Rest and calm should be the very foundation for the evolvement of mankind. Don't concern yourself about tomorrow, focus on the moment. Preprogramming from past generations and from the media has a lot to answer for and you need to see through all of that as much as possible. Life as you know it is changing and at times you don't see it because of the gradual movement in so many areas. When one part moves all the other parts follow; it's all combined and interwoven, like a fine network of connected beacons glimmering in the sky. There is so much in life and the universe and the Father created it all and it is all in his hands.

May you all help to send love and light back. TttA

THE UNIVERSE WILL PROVIDE!

How many times have we said so, and low and behold, it is so, it's not always what you think, but that's not for you to query. The Father is your helper, your teacher and your healer, so he provides the best possible solutions in the best and fastest way. So much more could and would be advanced if only you followed the path of obedience. Don't think of it as control though, its not, its about guidance. Later on as you begin to follow the path of obedience you will find it will take an even shorter time to discover the what, where and when to your questions. Everything is quite well organized and if you are willing to be more vigilant about order, you will find that the spirit can move in so many other different ways. Be open to the changes and slowly but surely all will be sorted, work for the spirit. The universal kingdom is the center of the father's realm and is mighty, eternal and reliable. When the spirit moves you, go, but check first, sometimes you will not know when it's true or false. So many of you are working for the light and you are creating an army of light bearers that will joyfully spread and pass on the truth about the love and light from us. There is no age limit for this work, we just supply the wisdom, strength and love. So start rejoicing, you are lovingly supported by us. TttA

ONCE AGAIN!

Once again you have to stand back and look at your situation. Nothing is wrong, it's just a temporary discomfort for a very short while, to get rid of old patterns and to think afresh. The unease you feel is just a part of you that wants to know what it is all about before hand, Stop that, Now! WE have promised that you will have everything you need, so leave that to us. You are now supporting yourself, as are so many others but you are always supported by us. It's hard for you because you have not always had that, so it takes time to change the thought patterns; for them to be activated, but it will be so, it's happening right now. You will experience so many differences when you let go and trust us to do the healing and repair work on you. You will co-create with the Father and start a new wave of hope and glory. It will happen gradually, but it will happen, so always hope, heal and help. Activation is a real and true way forward. Now you know a little more, so don't be too hard on yourself. Give praise and pleasure to yourself and to others. Enjoy your new music and alternate your rest with work, don't overdo or underdo anything. Blessings, a lot of help and healing, and most of all, hope to you.

Blessed be. TttA

MY CHILDREN TAKE HEED!

Please, take notice of the wisdom we give you and the healing and support from us, the angels are so willing to guide and assist you. It's a privilege for the ones that work for the universal spirit and the progress of mankind to have the two-way communication between us. You have asked for that so many times and we have never let you down, it's just that at times you have not had the wisdom to relax and receive, better times are coming for you. So much, in so many areas, has had to be uncovered and released so no wonder this last year has been so hard and strained, but now it's nearly done. Courage again my friend, you have bravely carried on, that shows us that you have patience, healing power and hope. Others might wonder what's going on with you at present, there is an internal process going on so bare with it, nothing is wrong, only a change of order and the strengthening of vital parts - disorder into order. That's our work so be glad that it's being done so that you can work for the good of all mankind on earth. Remember to keep the balance and give yourself some time to digest life and it's flow.

Love, health and wisdom. TttA

GLORY TO THE FATHER!

Remember to always give praise and glory to the Father, because without that interaction, things will not be so quickly activated, it's all to do with inflow and outflow. The pattern is so intricate that you would do well to follow through with what we give you, all living things are involved and get their life force from the Father, so let go, again and again. Store the wisdom and the love and light in your spirit bank, it is good to have when you are under pressure, in pain or dealing with previous lives. The storm today will bring fresh air and eventually a chance for the ground to dry, so it can ready itself for new growth. These things happen in stages and the same applies to your spiritual growth. First there is a letting go, then an uncovering of all that has been buried. At that point you can then ask for the lesson you need to learn and finally, you can ask for whatever it is that troubles you to be released forever, just don't ignore it, learn from it. Yesterday will then be gone, and we can carry on from there. Take care of today, and as you have not yet seen tomorrow, leave that to us. Don't take on anyone else's pain, sorrow or anger; it's not for you to deal with, the person involved has to deal with that. Show compassion by all means, but leave all their problems to us. You just need to relax, rejuvenate and rejoice at every possible moment. Today you will hear news from afar. Keep up the good work and more tomorrow.

Love and light. TttA.

HEALING AND STRENGTH!

Always believe that it is possible, especially if it is in the name of the Father. He holds the reins and at the moment all is in the correct order, all you have to do is listen and follow through. You don't need to despair - things will come right for you, all the little changes and all the discomforts you are experiencing will eventually vanish and never return. Yesterdays event was a big test for you and you passed with flying colours. You are learning but you can always learn more, we know what you are capable of doing, so be brave and believe in yourself. It all comes back to 'I am, I can, I will' and 'I believe'. You know that all areas will be dealt with in their own good time, so be patient, alert and never give up hope, if or when you think that there's no way out, leave it to us. Stop thinking or working out until tomorrow, it has been enough for you today. I can promise you 24 hours of relaxation, so be content and accept it, I will be your friend and companion throughout the day and night. So much depends on 'Me', so don't try to do things without us, you don't see the big picture yet because it is not yet complete but do your best in the meantime and we will do the rest.

Blessings, love, healing and support from your loving team. TttA

RELAX AND GET HEALED!

That's what we want you all to do. We can't get through to you when there's tension or worry, you would do better, if at times you just did nothing. For many, we know it's hard to just cut off, to just sit quietly in a natural state and soak up the healing light from us but if you study the animals, especially cats, you will find that the most natural way to go, is to go with the flow. By all means move about and stretch after sitting, but only in a gentle way. We understand that the way has been stony at times, but don't let that stop you; there is a way around those problems, as you will learn on your walks. The new music will also lift your spirits and heal old emotions. Trust, faith and heavenly love is still a big part of your learning. It needs time to build up; for it to get to a point where you can leave things to us, or where you will leave it to us to say when, but for now try to let go of wanting to know the outcome or exactly when. Take care of each day with a mixture of rest and work, the time now is meant to prepare you for future work. Your meditation night will also expand. Also let go of trying to understand your medical situation, it's in our hands now and we will help you to cope the best way possible. Healing is given every day.

Blessings and courage. TttA

STAY CLOSE TO THE SOURCE!

Yes my earthly children we need you to stay close to us. At the present time there is so much going on so you should try to stay clear of all that turmoil. Aim for peace no matter the cost. The ones that have disturbances of the soul will still get there, but first you must have our peace and calm in the very core of your soul. Stop and withdraw into your sanctuary for complete rest and recharging and when you are refreshed go out and teach, heal and enlighten the souls that are in a never- never land or mist. Believe and it will be done unto you. Your faith has improved and your spirit knows that all will be well. To be down in the valleys is understandable, but now you and many others are climbing to the top, it's a wonderful view; to be able to see the picture from above is indeed a blessing. The healing continues for you. Last night, right throughout the night, you received healing in every area that your body required or needed and it will continue like this for as long as you need and for as long as you think about it. Healing and love is only ever a thought away. We will send you all the love you need, trust us and have faith, keep on working as you are and you will experience and see true wonders unfold.

Blessings in full measures. TttA

NURTURING!

Spend time nurturing yourself and others, remember all living things need nurturing. Give them the love and light from your heart so that the life force gets through to them. No living things are so made that they can get by without it, they all need the input of love and the healing light to be able to stay healthy and well, so that means no stagnating on your part. Don't keep your input to yourself, share everything you have and you will feel invigorated and alive; today you will see proof of just that, all you have to do is ask and you will receive. If you don't get a response the first time, try again later. You are forever learning, forever growing but each time you learn something new or grow a little, your work for the light is that much better. To take a chance when it feels right is okay. Next week will bring you a lot of news and into contact with a lot of new people. This will enable you to connect more with family and with friends in so many new places. Persevere with other situations for a short while, there are temporary measures at work at the moment because of all the alterations going on inside your body, and also, out in the universe. Have patience and take care, with all our love.

Blessed be. TttA

COURAGE TO KEEPING ON!

Remember these words. We know how you feel at times; tired - very tired and just plain despondent. That's what happens when you don't have balance in your life; running on empty you might call it. How can you expect to do good works when you are depleted? Withdraw, recharge and get into the habit of doing nothing. Feel that we are around you, some of you might even see and talk to us, but you must remember to empty out so that we can fill you up with fresh vitality and a renewed spirit. No one gets away for long without suffering some sort of loss because of his or her actions, it all has to do with cause and effect. Watch how the garden grows. All is in order with the growth, but it needs tender nurturing and love. It is the same with humans, balance brings order into your physical life. Remember, all of your body's living cells are alive so talk to them, give them tender nurturing, love and light in full measure and wait and watch to see how your body responds. Let go of ingrained ideas, as they are not longer valid and bring some balance into your physical life. The Father made it all and with that comes the wisdom, health and security that you need. What more can you wish for. Faith, trust and love and in saying that to you, we mean real faith, real trust and real love.

Blessed be My earthly children. TttA

LET THERE BE LIGHT!

Now and forever, let go of all the darkness and dark thoughts. Yes, banish them for good. They don't belong to you or your place anymore. You were only picking them up from the world around you or from entities in the past and present and they were inhibiting you. Your shield is now so much stronger so they won't be able to enter through the light but ask for more light just to make the barrier that much more dense. You need protection at all costs so keep building it up so that you have a sanctuary for yourself and other people in times of strife. Shower love on yourself and on others, so many want too but don't always know where to find it or how too. You know, so tell them or give them the room to express it themselves in their own way. Watch and you will see their inhibitions banished and they will feel so much better. Also, you need to let go of worrying about tomorrow, that's for us to let you know about and when the time is right, you will hear. Check to make sure it's not someone trying to imitate us though. The Orion connection knows all about earthly ideas so watch and wait. Living in these changeable times is not easy but remember, easy does it. Because of your knowledge you will succeed with many. Send blessings to Mother Earth and it will help to heal all that pollution. Today you will experience another miracle. Blessings to you always my child of light, as well as help, healing and harmony.

Love and light. TttA

GOOD AFTERNOON!

We have been waiting for you the whole day. There is so much going on; cleaning, changing and at the same time new life emerging. Tell us when so we know. Tonight you will experience something new with whoever comes and we will be there to give you healing, recharging and light. The lady 'A' has now got the message not to overstay so you will have more time to do your work. Today's shifting of energy will be very beneficial for you just as giving away little things was very good for you. Soon the peace in your heart will stay and you will feel a lot calmer, the waiting is over, so make the most of it all. Remember to send love and light to all tonight. The student 'I' is still feeling the effects from yesterday, good for him. Support and guide, and open your home more and you will feel more alive and well, you are advancing so let it all unfold, we are behind you so trust, love and have faith. Thank you for trying so hard, it will bear fruit.

Eternal blessings. TttA

STORM AND UNEASE!

Don't be too disturbed by it all, as its all for the good. Soon it will clear and a better future will unfold. Next year a lot of souls will come back to you and your sanctuary and they will want to know how it will happen, that's up to us, you are still the go-between person and a good student, as we know. Carry out our wishes and we will then know exactly how much you are capable of doing. We have given you the strength and ability to work with our student, so use them well. At present the weather changes from one minute to the next, that's because of the universal alterations that are happening at present. The big picture is being remolded so let go of all the things that you can't do and let us take care of them. Don't blame yourself or take it personally, its because you humans are so made that you can pick up the vibrations from the universal changes and the sort out what is occurring. Just believe and unwind, we want you to know that we are working very hard to make all the changes as smooth as possible. My children, it is only a temporary situation and it will soon pass. Praise be to the Father that knows all and is in charge. TttA

ALL IN GOOD TIME!

Don't worry if you don't get everything done straight away, there are so many ways to do things, and the most practical is usually always the best. So much needs to be seen to, so make a plan that shows you how and when. The same goes for your spiritual progress, ask us for guidance.

Always put the spirit first and all other areas will be seen to, once again we need to remind you about order; about keeping calm and emptying out. Take one day at the time and you will soon understand why. The energy in your home is now sorted out, so you should start to feel better and brighter. Flowers, water and bells will help you also. Your 'changing about' today will be good for you, you know that all is well, so wait and carry on as we suggested, think happy calm thoughts when eating. All of last years of upheaval unsettled your digestion, but it's slowly coming back into balance. Your name change was good; the old ways are not for you anymore, so rejoice that is dealt with. Still, we do understand your concern, we are often with you now and one day you will see us. Ask for more miracles and you will be rewarded.

Eternal blessings and strength from us all. TttA

SUNNY GREETINGS!

Let my sun warm and gladden you - so much is growing, both inside and out, the water and sunshine will aid in all of it. Mother Nature is busy now with the awakening of all living things, a new season means new life is evolving once again. Learn from us and try to follow through, you know that's the best and fastest way for you, have no more concerns about your physical being, it's in our hands now so don't worry anymore. The more you evolve, the more your body will get rid of unwanted matter. Congratulations. You have worked that part out and you are also listening to us more, it's now easier to hear our thoughts, even through all the hussle and bustle, focus is a part of that, so keep focused. The stillness in your garden refreshes you and more and more you will understand that the last year has been for your own good. Thankfulness is also a big part of your release. To smile under such extreme circumstances is not easy, but you are learning. We still give you healing throughout the night, so it will be easier for you in daytime. Tension is now leaving your body, so keep up your work and all is well.

Love and support from us all. TttA

SUNNY GREETINGS ONCE MORE!

My children, we know how much you want warmth and sun; it's normal and very natural, all living things are recharged and enlivened by them. Storms and rain might come but you still have calm and peace. Your inside life is so much more important, so look after that first. Your light connects with the source and without that you can't be a lighthouse and let others know about the light. Some will ignore it and others will laugh about it but take no notice. You know who is who, let them go. You will soon have more interested souls coming but be patient and ask for the tools for the new connections. They are coming but you yourself need to unwind and lighten up more, and when you do, you will draw other like-minded people to you. Look at your thoughts and watch how often you get back exactly what you have sent out, you could probably do with trying to introduce more light-hearted thoughts into your system, this is only advise and you can do with it what you like, but don't act to soon. Some things take time but eventually they will come out okay. This week will be very interesting. Wait and see how much comes back to you. Smile.

Love from us all. TttA

GLAD TIDINGS!

Yes my child of light, the gladness is coming to you in full measure, it's the fruit of all your labours, still we say, go easy on yourself and others. Too much change in a short time can cause things to become untangled all too quickly, let everything unfold in it's own good time. Don't plan for tomorrow yet, so much is happening behind the scenes, so just go slowly. Enjoy the company of the right kind – the positive kind, unwind and relax and we will do the rest. We are watching over you so relax and allow your healing to speed up. Don't ask too many questions, they will only disturb you at this point. Trust, love and faith are still the best ways to get results, so go on with your day and smile a little more. Life is not that dull, even if you have had a lot to deal with lately, let go of all the 'if's and but's' and past happenings that have disturbed you. Now that you have changed your name, you're a new person and if you expect good things, good things will come to you, faster then lightning. Choose to be healed and it will be so.

Blessings and love throughout the day. TttA

GLADNESS NOT SADNESS!

Yes my children of light, practice just that, you would do yourself and others a favour if you did. So many are lacking joy and harmony and the reason is often unfinished ideas or business, not confronting life itself. To escape in such a manner is often the course of many sad times, but you don't have to deal with that; not all at once at least, one subject at a time and you will sort it out bit by bit. Today is a new day, so treat it as such. Yesterday was another learning time for you, about some of life's little confusions and connections, but go ahead today and enjoy what's coming your way and be glad that you can see so much love in the world. We know you better than anybody else, so believe that trust, love and faith will take care of all your needs. The universal storehouse is full, so claim some big things, and we will take care of it. At times you will have to wait, but that's not for you to decide about. There is an old saying that God is not always there when you want him, but he is usually there right on time. The same goes for the sun, it's always there, but at times we cannot see it because of clouds. Rest and keep calm for the rest of the day.

Healing and blessings from us all. TttA

THINK WELL AND YOU WILL FEEL WELL!

Ponder upon this truth; whatever your mind thinks, it will be. Your spirit is the strongest part of you but it isn't always in charge, it will be in time but for now, beware of too much monkey chatter; all it will do, is lead you up the wrong path and drain you of a lot of energy. Unfortunately for many it has become a bad habit because of the way they were taught when they were young, they need to empty out the old and then they can receive much more. Trust and do not be afraid, fear and pain are your enemies and there is no reason why you should have to deal with them. When you surrender to the source it will heal you and shield you from harm. Don't despair if or when you have to wait, some things take time and have to unfold slowly. Today is a day for cleansing, both inside and out and you need to recognize that it is a necessary development. Stay in tune and be patient, it will pass. Little hiccups will happen here and there but it's only your system coming into balance. Keep up your good work and just take one day at a time, don't look for an absolute answer just yet, we will let you know. Trust like a child.

Blessings and love. TttA

ALL IN GOOD TIME!

Don't rush around trying to change your priorities, 'Steady as she goes' needs to be your mantra for today. Good work takes time so stay patient, be vigilant and take a spell or time out in between things. Stand back and look at the situation so you can see what's going on clearly, at times you are so close to everything that you can't see clearly. Ask for input in any areas that you are struggling with, everything operates together and so if one area is not whole, nothing will balance. At these times stop, rest and ask for the remedy to your specific situation. Otherwise, as so often happens at these times, everything will get mixed up. You can look at problems, but don't give out an answer before checking with us. Remember, you are still learning and growing and you are just a vehicle for us to help pass on our wisdom and healing, you are the bridge. All of you have your part to do and you need to focus on that part. Splitting your energy is not good for anyone; it is just too draining. You need to build up your store-house and top up your spirit-bank for the times to come.

Blessings and courage. TttA

SUNSHINE AND ROSES!

Let's enjoy the sunshine and its warmth, its healing light and relaxing times. Mother Nature is so wonderful and always will be, so again, we say enjoy it. So many think of nothing but doom and gloom but that's just negativity, don't fall into that trap; so often it is being used as a 'side tracking' device and so you need to look closely at those situations. If it does feel right then by all means go with the flow. Tonight will be another chance for you to connect with your support team. Breath in the fresh air and listen to your birds, your wonderful garden will bring so much joy this year, so many will come and sit in it and be recharged and renewed. Some people will always try to intimidate or belittle you but they don't understand or know who you are. In those situations just detach and don't give them any energy, they will find somebody else to latch onto. It is better at those times, to stay in your 'castle' and only come out when it is all clear. Enough is enough! Ask us tonight for an answer and you will get it, go in our peace and do what's needed. Blessings and healing in many folds to you. Do not go back again, you have done your work well, every day.

Courage! TttA

COURAGE AND HOPE!

Yes, we know what's going on, so have courage my children. Everything will be all right, it's just that there is so much going on and a lot of it is just interference. So many are trying to put a spike in your wheel but it is to no avail, fortunately. You are the one that knows, others are only guessing or think they have it right, but you mustn't get involved in all of that, also, don't try to set a time for the change, it's been coming for some time now but first all aspects must be considered. Light a light and stop trying to work out the change for the photon belt, we have it in hand, but this year has to pass before you will see any marked differences. You need to be aware of false information also; so many think they have a message from the source, some do have, but for quite a few it is just that they want to give themselves an ego boost and hog the lime light. By now you should know who is a reliable and genuine source, just beware those who give orders instead of advice. There's a subtle difference, check as always and you will be okay. Some are not aware of their source, others are just naive to input, so stay firm, clear and very close to us and you will be cared for. Do claim more and we will come to your aid.

Eternal blessings and aid. TttA

ONE THING AT A TIME!

Yes my children, don't mix ideas or people up. They are all individual and you need to keep that in mind before you attempt to deal with anyone or anything. Today's hold up was another test. You laughed at it and that's a good idea, don't let anything on your planet disturb you. The only thing that you need to concern yourself with is spirit unrest, stop at once when it happens. You must identify it at once otherwise it will grow out of all proportion and will then require a lot of time and energy to sort it out. Learn from your animals, they are a part of nature and therefore very good at letting you know if and when something is not right. Learn to communicate with all living things and you will not go far wrong, practice until you get it right, this is why you need patience, proof and priorities. Keep on remembering our teachings and affirmations to remind you of our lessons. It takes time to change your thinking and to recharge, but in the end you will hear us better. You have improved a lot so keep the good work up. When you feel yourself getting tense, start laughing, that way you will not have any bad physical symptoms. Keep on learning, living and locating the truth.

Blessings. TttA

LET GO AND LET US!

Do just that. You don't know everything yet, but you are learning fast, just remember to take a break and refresh yourself every so often. Too much of anything is never good - a bit of balance is better for everyone, including yourself. Keep warm, smile and don't get tense about tomorrow, we will help you with that then. Let go of any mind disturbances. Your mind can be so powerful and it likes to always be in charge, but no more, your spirit has now taken over so you can rest assured your future is being cleared and you will receive more 'pictures' that will explain better what's going on. This process will save you time and energy and you will be able to better use them. Don't give up yet with your new communication device though, you have nearly got it, so persevere. If necessary ask us and we will keep you calm and focused. So many are making an effort and need our support and love, so we give it to you and you can then pass it on. Always remember to pass on our wisdom, love and cheer to all you come across. Your physical conditions are getting sorted, you just need to let us do our work and you do yours. Don't give any situation energy if we don't say to, determination is fine when the goal is right but otherwise just let it go. Blessed be and do let us know.

Love and light. TttA

STAY FIRM IN YOUR BELIEF!

My children, so much is influencing you at present but it's the same for many others who are being side-tracked and bewildered at present. There is truth amongst it all, but most of it is a mixture of ideas and various versions from so long ago. Learn to pick out the golden grains from peoples' lectures and let all other thoughts go. Because of your traditions and preprogramming, it can be hard to let go but we know you are doing the best you can and one day you will manage it. Ask us for guidance and healing for the next 24 hours when you awaken and it will be so. Order used to be a key word for you and you need to start using it again, it will save you time and energy. So much has changed for you and you need to accept that it is for the best, nature is waking up and so are you, Good! Take time out every second day - just have a little break, you now see more and so it can give you a greater hope, life force and love. Many are going to arrive at your door and you need to try and see why, often you won't know, so ask us for a clear 'line'. Let this month go and you will feel more invigorated, you can then go on to meet new situations in a better position. Keep up the good work.

Love and light. TttA

YESTERDAY IS GONE!

Don't re-live yesterdays interruption. It was more positive than negative and all in all you are getting there, it has taken a long time but it has been necessary for your type and system, it varies at times, but everyone has that problem. You are looking at so many areas at the moment and that is why you have had physical reactions, bear with us, and with yourself, it is getting better. We will stabilize you and make your 'field' more dense, don't worry about when it is going to happen, that's the main thing. The women 'A' is confused and lonely so leave her to us. Keep on building up your confidence day by day, there is nothing seriously wrong with you, just some old emotional battle scars and they are slowly fading. New information is coming, so take a little time to study what new possibilities there will be, just don't get too serious about it all, Just give it some thought. Try to take life a little more light heartedly and relax in between. As the weather gets warmer you will be able to go outside more often and just recharge. Smile and do your exercises as much as you can. More for you tomorrow.

Cheering thoughts and love. TttA

IN THE STILLNESS YOU WILL RECEIVE!

Stillness and calm will prepare you for new information from the source and you will be able to easily digest it, store it or give it out when it is wanted. Try to change the way you do things, the results will come faster and be better. Being practical is important but you need to find ways to operate with less energy and time being wasted. No one is ever too old, or too much of anything else, to look at new ways of doing things, accepting other options or being able to choose a different kind of life. It might take a while to alter patterns, but in time you will understand that it needed to be done, that it was a way to give a better kind of life to that individual. Mixing portions of this and that is not good, everything has it's own limits and it's own medications. Humans are so complicated so the healing we give you is given in the correct dosages and measures, all you have to do is relax and receive it. Don't try to operate on your own, it needs to be done in co-operation with the source of all life and when it is, so much life force will then pass through to you all. Well we will talk more again tomorrow. Rest and enjoy the rest of the day.

Eternal blessings and love. TttA

OUR FATHER!

Yes, he is also my father, we are one, let that message sink into your soul. Don't think too much or waste too much time on unnecessary actions, the simplest way is nearly always the best way. Let my light show you the way, it might seem at times that many think they have all the answers, but its much more involved than you think, so once again we say leave all that to us. Novices in this area would only cause a lot of work to have to be undone afterwards, so leave it to the experts. We are teaching you so that you can pass it on to others, so do just that. Remember what we have said so many times before; listen, learn and like what you hear. Don't think that you will learn everything in one day, a little at a time is best. Just as you did your homework when you were at school the first time, remember how long it seemed at times but when you finally got the picture all that was lost was that feeling of dread, and that is what's going on now. You will soon remember when you start to unfold your memory bank, the archaic records are still there and you can look in to them whenever you want to understand or know something. Cheerio for now and more tomorrow. Keep your life going.

Blessings and health. TttA

KEEP UP OUR WORK FOR THE LIGHT!

Never give up; just take a break in those 'in-between times'. All work requires order and energy and to have both is the ideal. You shouldn't try to hard to fit everything in, just do what is most suitable at the time, other peoples' priorities are not your concern. You need to concentrate on your own priorities and when you are asked, deal with that one thing at that time, life is about to change for you, so go with the flow. If and when technical misadventure appears don't spend too much time on it, leave it and go back to it later, if you need to ask for advice, ask, and we will help you to find the right solution. Go ahead with your new input, it might just surprise you how much better and lighter you'll feel, as you evolve you will eat different foods, habits might alter and the way you feel will stabilize a lot more. Last night, and today, you connected with the Egyptian and because of that meeting old wisdom's will be used again for the benefit of many. You are here to support and help each other and to love one another, by that we mean real love, not the make believe one, all that's not real has to go, a much far better life will come of real love.

Carry on as you have started and we will continue to send you our blessings, our eternal blessings on your path ahead. TttA

LET GO OF LITTLE HICCUPS!

Ignore these things at all cost, they are there to cause hold-ups or to make you worried again. I say ignore them all. Stop and get all the facts straight, ask us where from and everything will fall into place, most times costs are involved, so ask for more input. Go ahead with your plans today and it will eventually turn out alright, soon it all will be forgotten and you will see why it went the way it did. The weather also has a new face, it is too cold for this time of the year with snow and hail. You might ask what next, but it will clear and you will feel the peace and joy that follows. The whole universe is altering because of the re-alignment and also because other solar systems are involved. My Father is still holding on to the reins, just relax and let us carry out our work. The strain is started to show as all concerned are overloaded with work at present, smile at it all whenever possible. All the 'N' forces need at present is energy, so that's why we are reminding you about love and laughter, that will relax you and stop the energy flow from you to others. Rest and you will reap the rewards once your physical body has settled down. Keep up your deep breathing and all will be well.

Blessings and love with health. TttA

JOY AND WISDOM!

My children of the light, you all are our joy and we are delighted to give you our wisdom. We are eagerly watching your progress and every little step ahead you take, climbing upwards, is music to our ears. Such a long time has past, but at last we meet again. You and your fellow light workers are doing your part to lighten up the Earth so stay steadfast and vigilant, it's not an easy life, it was not meant to be so, but you need to learn and see. To become a fore-runner takes courage and stamina, carry on as you are, and take only one day at a time, you can't see tomorrow yet so just enjoy today. The same goes for your new weather patterns, they're coming and going at present, but it will stabilize into just one season in the future, it will enable you to change growth patterns and life will be much easier. Your life will be so much easier when all is settled, so play your music and enrich your life as much as possible until then. Still, stay connected to the source and keep receiving our nurturing, and most importantly, don't get carried away with your earthly dimensions.

Love and light from us all. TttA

HEAVENLY HOSTS!

Look up and feel the connection. Many are surrounding you and your work and all you have to do is ask and in an instant they will be present. The book you are reading at present will explain a lot more to you. You have wanted to read that book for a long time but not felt inspired to do so, finally you did it and the connection is very real, you will be able to draw from all that wisdom whenever you want now. Today will be a revelation day, you have now completed another chapter. It's hard for you at times because of your sensitivity, everything is magnified, to feel so deeply is a gift but it comes with a price. Your gift will be beneficial when working with others, so thank the universe for it. Remember in stillness you will find peace; play your music and know that the Tibetan chimes are dispersing any negativity. Leave the physical detail to us, your renewal is on its way so keep on trusting, loving and having faith. All your connections from the light are coming closer, so welcome them into your home with all the love in your heart. Delight in your work and try to smile a little more, you are being healed, loved and cared for and remember, when you give out love and healing we will always refill your vessel.

Blessings and love. TttA

MY DEAR ONES!

You all are very dear to us, we your teachers, guides and masters send you our love and support, so know that you can go ahead unafraid, don't let anyone or anything stop you. Many will try at this point to tempt, interfere or attack you at your weakest point, so guard your back and remember to start afresh every day. Yesterday is truly gone, so let it be. Stay disciplined, do your tasks each day, keep up your water intake and do your deep breathing, it will benefit you and others throughout your day. In the morning stillness you have the chance to invigorate all parts of yourself, every organ in your body is linked and they should all co-operate, their function is to serve the whole body. Don't rush around, go about things calmly and efficiently and you will succeed in getting done what has to be done, stay flexible. Don't listen too much to the media, the picture they show you is not the whole one, it's generally about politics or manipulation, so keep that in mind when you read or listen to it. Today will reveal something that you have been wondering about for a long time and a lot of others areas are going to be dealt with, It's on its way so keep on with your 'sort out' and keep up your loving.

All our help, guidance and love. TttA

GREETINGS!

Let our sun shine upon you and yours, it will warm, enlighten and revive you. Remember the old saying - the sun is always there even when you can't see it, the same goes for me, I am always there even if you can't always feel me nearby. You have come through a storm and you're still feeling the hustle and bustle of it, but now less so than before. As your light inside grows, so will your spirit life, so stay calm, be joyful and rest assured that all is indeed well. There are some that will offer other versions but don't listen to them, they should deal with their own spirit growth instead. Don't judge them, just make your own observations and learn from them. Go ahead with your tasks today, we will support you and because of our support you will feel better, keep on asking for miracles and trust that it will be so. Nothing is impossible for me, in days of old there were many miracles performed and that still applies today, miracles still heal. Nothing is really new, it's just that some things change so that you can better understand, it's just another facet of the diamond that we can look at. The same goes for other truths, sometimes it doesn't help to explore too deeply as it can only change the way it might be being presented, ponder on that and you will see more clearly. Take heed and all our blessings go with you.

Blessed be. TttA

MORNING HAS BROKEN!

After the darkness of the night you will feel the sunrise, even if you don't see it, it's just a part of the pattern and the law of nature. But before the darkness, before going to bed at night you need to remember to ask for answers to any unanswered questions or queries you have. Most of the time now, you are resting better so we are able to get through to you easier. Remember, the more relaxed you are the better our healing will be for you. During the day use your garden to relax, go out into it and enjoy it with friends who visit, whether they can be seen or not. The colours and healing vibrations from your animals and plants will aid everyone that comes to you. Last nights clearing was very beneficial for you both, how simple things are when you leave it to us and you're relaxed, afterwards you always feel more energized and far less tense. Unfortunately, many still try to tell you what, when and how, why do they bother when you don't even ask? Don't listen, cut the ties and get on with your days work. Outside feels great today even if it's not quite as you would like, however inside peace is your first priority, only then can you give out more of yourself to others, and as you do, we will give you more to give out, everyday.

Blessings and joy from us all. TttA

LET GO AND LET GOD THE FATHER!

Work as we bid you, don't ever try to clean, organize or decide things without our guidance, it could just do you some harm. For us to work together in the best way possible means that we need to care, love and protect you. You all have a specific learning curve and you would do well to stick to it, time is still of the essence, so use it wisely, allow yourself rest in between but afterwards start afresh. Give thanks to all your teachers, healers and angels. Beware of so called psychics and 'make-believe' healers, they are only pretending and are not committed, leave them to us but keep an eye on their eyes, the eyes always give them away. There are really only a few that are in this line of work in order to continue the light-work, money seems to drive a lot of the others to look at it in another way, so stay steady and only let the force of the wind bend you. Relax, smile, let others think exactly what they want, what they think is not your concern. All you have to do is stay clear of all the garbage and wait for our requests, to be patient and calm is more important than you think so follow through and keep up the good work. Blessings and help will come to you in full measure, the exposure was not nice, but it was a part of the learning once again. Be vigilant!

Eternal blessings to you. TttA

IN THE STILLNESS OF THE MORNING!

Let's all remember just that. Remember the feelings in the early hours of a new day, being able to breath in the fresh air, able to renew the feelings of being alive. Watering is a big part of that renewal and just as people want and need nurturing and love, they also need 'watering', you can show your love by doing for yourself and others, just that. Stagnant energy is not good for any living thing, it's the circulation of a positive life force that's so very important, but check who is sending it. In these times you should all be very alert, but not afraid. Let nature be as it was intended, don't poison or cut out too much, give the trees and birds a chance, clearing things is fine but don't prune too harshly. Play music and enjoy the harmonious vibrations, it will promote growth, health and well being. Today will unfold as it should, just try to stay clear of negativity and take what comes as lightheartedly as possible. Spend time outside and feel all that good energy, don't push anything or anyone, letting things unfold naturally is best. All our love goes with you in the name of the light.

Blessed be. TttA

JOY AND JEWELS!

These are two very valuable solutions you can use every day, we're not talking about earthly jewels, but that doesn't mean that they can't still play a part in many earthly situations. Joy means deep emotional, spiritual, mental and physical powers all combined into good energy and to be able to combine all four will emphasize the whole. To combine all four as a whole will make you much stronger so try to feel and enjoy as much as you can every day. You could find a jewel in the lowliest of places or in a palace. To be able to appreciate the shine and the shape of gems is fine but you need to know that you can also use them in your healing work, that's another thing with jewels. With jewels you can feel and see love that comes from the heart and even loyalty from friends. See it as we do, look into the very soul of a person and you will see the beauty that is mostly hidden there. Just ask, we will knock at the door and it will open so that you can share all that beauty and love with others. So many broken hearts can be healed with the help of gems and love. To be able to feel and see the smiles again on someone's face after a healing with jewels is a great joy and quite heavenly. The world of today will look quite different when so much is gone, so you all would assist us by loving and caring for your jewels for the sake of mankind.

Love and healing to all. TttA

SURRENDER TO THE SOURCE!

You all seem to like to know that you are in charge and yes it's true that freewill does still operate, but when the day begins you would do well to surrender to us and ask for guidance, healing and wisdom. The big picture is coming to you slowly, but in the mean time keep doing your daily tasks. Don't try to work out what's what too much, ask us again for advice, we want you to listen in, but first you need to empty out, how can we give you more when your head and soul is already filled with yesterday's woes? Even if you have had more than your share of woes lately, there have also been a lot of joyful events, just don't dwell on the pattern too much, it's on its way to being resolved. The universe is full of teachers, healers and scribes to name a few so take time-outs when you need them. Too much energy coming in means you need to adjust to your system, your patience and discipline is still in need of a little more fine-tuning. You are getting better at you practicing so keep it up, stay close to the source today and go along with our teachings. Your visitors today will bring you some news, to help you to understand the picture.

Blessings and love. TttA

SURROUND YOURSELF WITH LIGHT!

My Children of the Light, make sure that you are in the light and going towards the goal, so much depends on you. At times it would be so easy for you to just give in or to have negative thoughts but if you stay in the light you will be okay, just be aware of being sidetracked and stay alert. These things are happening because there's so much confusion about these days and that's because of the alterations going on in the universe. It affects all people on earth but especially the sensitive ones and those that have advanced and now work on a higher frequency, also beware of physical symptoms that appear out of nowhere, any changes of mood or ideas at this point would not be good for you. Don't give into temptations or start asking the questions "why me?" or "why not?" You need to disperse any action, thought or mind power that is negative straight away otherwise it will just fester and take much longer to deal with. Yesterday's confusions happened because of negative interference and other sticky operations. Be cautious, don't mix or mingle too much, it might even be to everyone's benefit to be reclusive and stay away from situations that will not benefit you. Go further up your climbing ladder and we will be on stand-by for a while.

Go on your path. TttA

GLAD TIDINGS!

Every day is a new day, so treat it as such. You should remind yourself at all times that that's what happened then, so learn from it and pass on what you have learnt. There's always a reason for what was, and it will come around again if you don't learn. Sometimes it will take a while before the red thread becomes clear to you, you won't always know where it is coming from or where it is going to, don't pick up any odd colours in these matters, otherwise it will just end up a tangled web. Life still goes on and people will be people, some learn faster than others, but that's not your concern, you are doing more than your part at present. The warmer days are here now, so go outside whenever possible you need the sun and fresh air, you can rest assured that you will be undisturbed and safe in your energy-giving garden, but be aware and keep your eyes and ears alert. Your garden will soon provide for many more so take things as they come, don't concern yourself with the shifts and change's, as things will settle down. You are still being tried and tested, so keep on working to see through people and situations, that way all other issues will be minimized.

Blessings to all concerned. TttA

ONE STEP AT THE TIME!

To build your spirit fort takes one brick at a time but in the end it's worth it, as it's a good place to have on stormy days or as a retreat. As protection it will bring you safety, peace and the opportunity to recharge so that when you go on your way, you can fulfill your destiny and at the same time feel joyful about it. At times you forget to smile, or even worse, laugh, that's because there's too much energy tied up inside you - you need to let it out through healing, love and laughter. Remember also to give yourself time to just do nothing. Today is an inside day, it's so cold and wet outside so do your work with us today. Yesterday was a day for clearing out old negativity and stale situations, so today should be a day for doing something for yourself, as long as you remember to give love and support to others. Send out health and love in all directions to those wondering why and how life will unfold. There are many people that have entities that have taken up refuge in their bodies and those entities will not leave their 'hotel' unless that person asks for a clearing to be done, it has to be done, but only if the 'landlord' asks. Be very clear about that, no one should tell another person what to do, it must come from the heart of the person. Wait if we say wait.

Blessings and wholeness for you today. TttA

LET THE SPIRIT FLOW!

Yes that's what we want you do, nothing is better than a spirit that soars up to us in the universal kingdom. We will rejoice with you and your fellow light-workers when one more soul comes free from bondage and wants to learn about the source of all life, so rejoice with your heavenly hosts whenever a little more work is completed. Don't think of yourself as having to organize all the work, no one on Earth is in charge. It is us who are in charge, we work through you and that is why we call you a bridge-worker, make yourself available and we will prepare the ground and give you the tools. Many people are "pearls in shell's" – so let it all come out and shine, likewise, 'pearls of wisdom' are not meant to be hidden or neglected. A pearl starts out as a grain of sand in the in sea and ends up shining in glory, it stays nestled in the safety of the shell's cocoon until finally the shell opens, then it can be fully enjoyed. So go out and let people know, old wisdom comes to light again, nothing is really new, it's just that things have been turned over or cleared away. So many pieces of wisdom have been hidden for so long. The Ethiopian has the light of Christ in his eyes.

Smiles from all of us. TttA

GO EASY ON EVERYONE!

That includes you also, it's okay to do so much work as long as you have an equal amount of time-out also, but working till all hours will not benefit anyone, so much more can be done when you follow a pattern of balance. At times an interesting subject carries you away, but to achieve a more quality standard of work you need to regularly stop and start, it just comes down to that word - BALANCE. Your meditations are fine, we always come when you ask and we are supporting, guiding and renewing you. Go along with today's plan and rejoice that it is finally happening. You will get further along your path today but listen in and we will give you all the extra tools that you need. In the stillness of the morning you will find peace, so stay outside a little longer, walk amongst the living plants and soak up their energy, you all need to refill once in a while and Mother Nature is still the best healer, so use her. So much help was given to quite a few yesterday, so many thanks from all the many souls that were finally released to the light. Thanks also to Anarama for the tears of joy and freedom from bondage.

The searching souls send their blessings, eternal love and light to all concerned, keep up the good work. TttA

KEEP ON, KEEPING ON!

It's always darkest before the dawn, it's what we have said many times before and it is still a very valid analogy. Don't make any big changes at present, there is too much going on and too much confusion. Big decisions need a great deal of calm and peace, just go on with your daily tasks, for as far as we are concerned, doing the little things also shows obedience. Trust, faith and love are the basic ingredients for all of mankind. Let the day unfold and you will be surprised to find at the end of it that everything turned out well. There are so many negative thought patterns about at the moment and also some very strong entities doing their best to sidetrack or bewilder everyone and all because panic buttons have been pressed. The confusion has disturbed many of them, but last night was a time for exposing these entities. The people there reacted to the ringing of bells and other sounds, but it wasn't the person reacting, rather the entity that was inside them. The entities became scared and didn't want to leave and therefore you heard yells, and saw them act out of character. That's your alarm signal, act at once or better still, ask us and we will deal with it, when we are finished wash, clear and cut. The big white artificial cloud you saw last night was another sign that we are supporting you so don't give up now, your goal is in sight. Courage my friend.

Love and light to you all. TttA

GREETINGS!

We greet you and yours with love and light. We know why you of all people react like you do, such a sensitive system takes a lot of getting used to. It's why you understand others so fast, however you mustn't concern yourself with all of the various human conditions, they will take care of themselves. The only thing you need to spend time on is spiritual matters and your own understanding and growth, some will try to trip you up, but you must keep information about yourself and your work as quiet as possible. Understand that they would love to get you out of the way, even though it's useless them trying, they don't know you as well as we do. Today was a good example, but you will see even more examples soon. A lot of energy has changed since your shifting, even your helper has done her bit to aid you, she is coming on fine so send her love and light, she will benefit from it, as will the HN man, so much skepticism but that's healthy. Don't push anything or anyone too hard, rather call them in your mind instead of from your spirit, you should do this from now on.

Loving support from us. TttA

PEACE UPON YOU ALL!

Peace on Earth is one of the first things that you must work on, without that nothing can be activated.

Try taking a second look at what's going on around you and soon you will start to realize that you can recognize different souls and signs. So many do not know who is in charge and how to get rid of energy. For those people you will have to explain it to them in very simple terms, using their own language as much as possible, even using parables if you have to. Soon mixing with others will get easier, but only once your buffer zone is thicker, it is then that you will be able to move freely everywhere. Entities will still try to get in but when they can't they will try things like physical disturbance. A person's weak side will always be hit first, so a thick buffer zone is important. Each time they try they will be sent back to the source of love and light. This kind of monkey business doesn't need to exist, however these poor, lonely and unhappy souls don't want to go back through the tunnel into the light because of their fears, guilt and possible punishments. You need to give all that to us and go ahead with your day, but keep your eyes and ears open. Special thanks to all of you that help and work for the light.

Blessed be. TttA

HEALING FROM THE INSIDE!

Yes my children, it must start from the inside, the healing light comes in through the top of your head and goes to where it's needed inside you. It's there to be used and to make you whole, so again we bid you to sit down, empty out and when you are relaxed, we can refill your vessel. We have told you often enough how important it is to empty out first, but most people do not understand this fully and they wonder why they don't hear or see more. It appears that someone is trying to convince you or tempt you into a change of attitude. You are going to need a lot of energy from the source to be able to stand your ground, so let my light and love re-invigorate you and strengthen you as a whole being. It might even be a good idea to study the negative forces, they are some of the subtlest tactics that you will ever come across and you need to be aware of them. You may even have to use them in an opposite way – like a lot of things they can easily be used two ways. They will make you think about what you are doing at all times, but let nature take it's course, don't struggle against the wind. Start your paintings again and we will speak through them.

Blessings to all of you, always. TttA

PEACE UNTO YOU!

Let our peace fill your soul to the very core and then spread out to others. All peace must come from the source and we know you know, so tell others. It's no use keeping that knowledge all to your self, one way or another people hunger for that, that cannot be brought. Material things are things to be shared, but it is more important to share spiritual truths and knowledge. The weather is chopping and changing, as are people so stay clear of them and try to keep calm and stable, ask us for some extra input and energy if you need to. Take each day as it comes and ask for miracles, they still happen just as they used to such a long time ago, you know how much you need them, so call and we will contact you, don't ever despair and be sad, everything is under control. So much good is going on and yet so many are hit after doing good work, but we will strengthen all of them so that they can hold on and do as much as possible, have courage my helpers, cheer each other up and offer support where you can. Last night was the start of a long friendship, it will serve the source well but at times you will need to recharge.

We will send thoughts to the soul of 'I' and he will find the strength and discipline he needs, carry on as you are, thank you. TttA.

CALM IN THE MIDDLE OF THE STORM!

Try to understand, to bend is not to break. Enjoy being flexible and being able to stand firm and straight after bending, otherwise you can easily become stuck in a position. So it is the same with your spirit life, don't let things stagnate, the stale energy will only make you grow old, ask us for input and let the sun shine upon your face and penetrate your whole being. It's like watering the garden, the water needs to penetrate the plant's surface, otherwise they will die and so you need to allow the sun to penetrate your whole being and water your spirit with the living water from the living source. Forget old tales about doing everything by the book, according to your ancestors there is a spiritual way to always follow through with what we suggest. Society is so mixed up so you must ask how can the so called rulers give you eternal advice, the laws of every country will alter in time, but always be aware of who is in charge. So many sheep are wandering around on stony ground, but always looking for a fertile meadow, that is what temptation does to you. The big illusion is apparent everywhere and many buy in to it, don't you, look behind the curtains, stay alert and look deep into things.

Blessings of light to you all. Ttta

GLORY TO GOD!

Remember to give all the glory to God for it is where all the wisdom, strength and life force comes from - you are just the vehicle through which the force for eternal good works. To be able to work together like this is always the best form of exchange, to only take is not good for anyone's development. Life is about learning balance, everyone has to learn it and while it's not always easy for some, it will be easier for you. The same applies to animals and to the weather, the principal is the same, it's about achieving a balance and at present the vibrations and feelings are quite unsettled because of atmospheric disturbances. You need to leave any sudden pain or unexpected interference that may arise on the horizon to us, we know the answers and you are just too involved to try and find an answer yourself. To try and do too big a task to soon is not wise, in your case it is better to do things gradually, take a 'gently does it' approach and you will get through. Yesterday's storm stirred things up but also cleared some other things out, rest assured you are well guarded and protected and if you do happen to feel uneasy, stand back, or perhaps, try to do something practical, the main thing is to focus on a task. It's time to start smiling again and to let us be there for you all day.

All our help guidance and love. TttA

NURTURING IS A GOOD SIGN!

Yes, you of all people know that to weed, water and fertilize is so important for good growth and that without it everything wilts, it's an everlasting quest and the season will soon tell you if you've been successful. In the future you are only going to have one season and you will start to grow other new plants, the season will be split between dry winds and rain. Crops for eating will produce greater harvests, more tropical plants will bear fruit and more people will be employed. The type of farmers and people that work in this industry will alter, prices will come down, plants will have more health benefits and give more life force to everyone. In the beginning there will still be some chemicals used, but eventually there will be none, it will eventually become totally natural. Many long forgotten remedies will start to be used again and you will start to see herbal remedies sit along side traditional medical remedies. Even sound vibrations will start to be used to help alleviate medical conditions, most of today's problems come from the way we think and live, so a change in our belief systems needs to happen. Start to take heed of things and slowly start re-evaluating your systems and what's good for what.

Blessings and peace to all. TttA

NEWNESS!

Yes my children of light, it can be done each morning as you awaken, it just needs faith. Your spirit goal is you, so let go of old ideas about life, the things that you learned a long time ago are not right for today's world. The validity of much of it has changed, however don't throw out the basic sound techniques, you can still apply them to today's life. So much has happened in those in between times and sometimes it's hard to sort or sift things properly, but you are getting better at knowing what to do and your ability to understand is improving. There are still many situations that you need to look at more carefully but you have seen the main ones. Some require little changes to be made here and there, but generally a lot of them are just another version of a similar thing. When you have climbed higher you will have a better view of everything, so apart from stopping for little rests, keep learning. It will take time to digest it all but as you learn you will become more aware of how it all works. Try not to compare your path with someone else's, that would be of no good use to you at all. Wishful thinking is okay, but just as long as your motive is clear and it benefits your higher self. Let today bring you joy and blessings. Thank you to all.

Courage and health. TttA

OBEDIENCE!

Our father wants obedience but don't be worried - he has everything in hand so you will be safe letting go of your 'if's and but's'. You may wonder at times but that's only because there is so much going on around you. Sometimes you can feel quite rattled and consequently your physical being will pick up on that unease, we are working to help you to detach from those particular feelings. Your heart goes one way, the brain another and it has to stop! Neither of them is in charge, it's your spirit that is and they would do well to accept that, the changes will be very subtle but they will be for the best, remember 'I Am', how many times have we reminded you about that? Take time out and just be, so should others, otherwise the strain will start to show up and your body will react accordingly. Again we say to you 'Don't compare', you all have lessons to learn and we will always be there for you. Let your garden refresh you, and others, its energy connecting you with the most wonderful healer on Earth, Mother Nature, she comes from the source, from the beginning, like all of you. Your home is always open to us. Thank you. Today's quest is to be calm and joyful, no interruptions of a negative nature, please.

All our blessings and love, now rest in our knowledge. TttA.

STORMS MIGHT RAGE!

When you are connected to the source you will never fall, you may bend but you won't break, you of all people know that. It just comes down to being flexible and going with the flow, you won't stagnate when you're like that. Some people react to disturbances or have different opinions to you but you mustn't follow the masses. Stay by yourself if you have to, your convictions and your faith, which is strong in you, will get you through. Let things be if your spirit says to, move only when you feel things are right and you will find it's all a part of a chain of events that are working closely together. While some do one thing, others do another but for you the will to get there will be your faith. Love and trust are the other main ingredients that will enable you to learn and advance. Once you have the basics we will fill in the rest for each soul. Sit and ponder when you need to and reflect on your lessons. At times your patience has been tried to its very limits but its only when you stop and reflect that you can see what's what. It's like walking through a desert, you have to prepare for what you will need and then proceed in stages, having breaks when you need and then going on. It is the same with your journey through life, look at it as a lesson, do your homework, keep going and see it for what it is.

Your teachers and guides are always there to help. TttA

TO KNOW WHEN IS TO BE WISE!

Let us teach you more about 'when' and 'how', as just knowing is not always enough, the real wisdom is in knowing how or when to give or receive. Generally it's best to wait until all the conditions are just right, so you need to learn to just wait. At times you start to get impatient with your work but that's understandable, there are so many situations that you are dealing with at the moment and each one is different to the one before but you are starting to respond faster and clearer to them. Some may not agree but that has nothing to do with you. There are people out there that need the focus on them and to get that they will make as much noise as possible or throw a tantrum of sort, they do that because they don't want to deal with what is on their own pathway. Human nature is so complex so stand back occasionally and reset your boundaries. Its no use explaining to them what is going on, as they would not understand, leave that to us to do, as we will know when their spirit is ready. Go along with today and try to relax, listen to your music. Unfolding times are here at the moment, you will see this happening more and more, it's been a long time coming and as you make a connection everyday, you will feel it. Also your ear problem will get sorted. Thank you for the work you have done, keep it up.

All our love and support. TttA.

YESTERDAY IS GONE!

Please don't hold on to the happenings of the past or yesteryears, it's no good for you, today is a new day so treat it as such. Ask for protection, a good shield, and because needs keep changing check in with us more than once a day. Rest and relaxation needs to be a big part of you life, so don't let interruptions hold you up, lock the door if you have to, it's your door to lock, so just be firm. There will be time later on for the other things you have to do and you will get through them. Stay clear of negativity, people programmes and the news media, they are tools of 'the system' to programme the masses, it's very skilled and it works very well, getting people predisposed to a new way of thinking and how they are supposed to live their lives. It doesn't make a lot of sense to many people but when you see and understand what's going, on you will work harder to stay clear of it all. Let us take care of your connections, have a break and recharge and if anyone asks for input just pass it on to us, you have enough to look after at the moment. As you know, too much of anything is never beneficial, it all comes back to balance, ponder on that and smile.

Courage and blessings to you all. TttA.

CATCH UP TIME!

Time goes by so quickly when so many subjects come at you at once, so don't allow that to happen, try to separate them and deal with just one subject at a time according to our wisdom. You need to listen in more and start to feel what needs to be done and how. Last night was a little uneasy but it was like that to test you and the others, it was nothing major but it proved you are getting better at focusing and letting go. The respect that was discussed is fine but remember it must come from both parties. Today you need to let the stillness of your garden put some harmony and peace back into your life, stay vigilant as someone may try to disturb you and yours, just be prepared. Today's sun will energize you so take advantage of it and go out and allow it to soak into your body and soul. There is nothing really wrong with you, what you are experiencing are mind tricks and at times they come to test you and to remind you who is in charge. It's so easy to forget the little things, especially given the way time tends to go so quickly and also how so many tend to change their mind to suit themselves. Confusion is in the air but don't you get caught up in it. Be a mediator and teacher but remember that all of your knowledge comes from us. Keep an eye on your environment and look to the sky at night, the next shift is much closer. A word of advice for you - stay firm with AS.

Love and light from all of us. TttA.

A NEW DAY!

Everyday is a new day, yesterday has gone as has the yesteryears so don't look for revenge or explanations, they are best left alone in the past. Sometimes sudden thoughts may appear clearly to you and they will enable you to understand what's been going on for so long. Things are not always as they seem, so be very careful before you make any kind of a statement, leave that to us and if necessary we will supply the tools and the wisdom. Life at the present time is very changeable and not what you are used to so let the events that are happening around you, teach you. Look and try to understand how to handle the different situations. Let our wisdom be known and speak your mind to all that we send you. The woman 'A' is still in a mist about what is happening but she must learn to understand how you want things around you, respect is called for from both directions. Remember to be honest, respectful and a good listener, good advice is to be listened to. Maybe as more people speak their minds many unnecessary situations will be avoided and there will be a lot more improved communication. Carry on with today's work and let the sun warm you and brighten up your day.

Lots of love and light to you. TttA.

PEACE AND HARMONY!

So much depends on the state of your spirit, mind and emotions, most of you are in a similar state but there are some amoung you that are at a higher level than others. That does not matter at the moment as there are areas that you are lacking in and they need work. They shouldn't be ignored, you know that better than most people, you have seen many people act as though it doesn't matter but it does. To grow is to advance but you must not hurry, it must come naturally. Don't ever be talked or pressured into change by anyone, they will have alternative motives and often it will be to do with their own areas of neglect. You have heard, seen or felt things about all of these subjects over the years but again we say study further and deeper, the course of events that have occurred over the last few days has opened your eyes even wider and therefore your contacts with the spirit have to be worked on. You have seen, but mostly felt it, so keep on learning how to identify who is who. It will sometimes appear as a true connection but always ask again if the source of contact is from the light, if it isnt send it away to the light. Your friend is also working on the same lesson and he will eventually get into a new order of life, give your support and love to him. Today you have to work with the spirit so ask clearly for what you want.

Blessings to all. TttA.

SORT OUT TIME!

It would be advisable to sift and sort things now as it will save much time and energy later, preparation time is beneficial to most people. Order used to be a key symbol to you so many life times ago and that still stands now. At the moment you are inclined to leave situations that aren't valid at present, that's fine, but you do need to keep your priorities in order. Don't forget to unwind in between things either, that way you will be able to know at any given moment in time what's needed. That's why you have an orderly mind but watch out – it can get out of hand. Don't try to be perfect for everybody all the time, just do what you think is best for you at that moment in time, as always you are only responsible for yourself and your growth, pets included. The advice we give you is real and you can trust us, unlike so many humans that think they know what, when and how. You are waiting for next years input and it will come soon enough, in the meantime carry on with your tasks and do your best. Next years group will be refreshed with new input and visions so cheer up. When unease is in the air take a break and ask us to calm everything down, trust and hope will get you through till then.

Peace be with you today and always. TttA.

THE SUN IS ALWAYS THERE EVEN IF WE DON'T ALWAYS SEE IT!

This is the way of so many other things to and at times you are just too close to a situation or to the people involved to see what is going on and you just need to stand back abit. The same applies to spirtual truth as well, do your meditation, but be relaxed in our company so that you can see and hear the wisdom that we are giving you, before starting always empty out, otherwise we cannot fill your vessel. Many think or say that they cannot hear or see anything and because of that they start to think that they are not advancing but that isnt so, it's just that they have too many things going on in to many places and it hinders the message. When that occurs let go but try to stay in our midst for a recovery time. You only ever have to ask for help or a visit from us and we will be there in an instant but the connection is all important and you just need to practice more. Big changes are near and will give love, light and support to all those that I send you, you will receive the tools and the ability to use them and the more you surrender the quicker the healing will take place. In the meantime keep playing your music, it is soothing to your soul when so many want your time and energy. Give some, but keep some.

Blessings and light to you. TttA.

RAYS OF LIGHT AND LOVE!

You all need a vigourous refill when your work has been done for the day and the rays of light and love outside are a great way to heal and renew. Go out into your garden of delight and just be, let the sun work its vigour on your human form; in the privacy of your garden absorb the light and love unabashed and as you do so, reflect on the fact that light and love and the delights of your garden are a good reminder of life and where it all comes from. Of late you have been experiencing new thoughts and a renewed strenght to carry on, this is all a preparation for the next step, whats left of your old life will go and will eventually be replaced with a higher level of knowledge so stay calm and firm at all costs. You are recovering from the stresses and drainage of your close living situation but remember it has been a learning situation for you about a different set of boundaries. Some will never listen or pay attention to what you are saying and so will carry on as usual, it is then that you need firmer ways to deal with them. So far so good, we will help you to control the comings and goings, your physical form is fine, it's only problem has been stress and wear and tear, so settle down and enjoy life a little more and what it has to offer. Courage and health is all yours.

Lots of laughter and eternal joy to you. TttA.

ENJOY THE DAY!

Yes, make the most of today and find something to be happy about, it doesn't need to be a lot, it need only be a smile or a phone call to let you know that someone cares. Trust us to put the thought into the head of whoever needs to contact you and they will, they might not realize that we have done it, but that doesn't matter. Try to see the purpose of it all, see that it's all just a network of thoughts, ideas and activations and let it lighten your load as well as ours. The present clean out you are having will leave room for new input and a turnover of energy and love. As you know stagnation is never a good thing, if something hasn't been used for a long time it possibly has outlived its usefulness so pass it on, it might be very handy for someone that's wanting material or to keep occupied. You will find that as life goes along it requires change and so you must move things on to the next place, but at the same time keep an eye on happenings around you. Don't alter your actions before you are ready, its called divine timing and that means that things are only meant to happen when all concerned are ready. It would be wise to accept that thought, unexpected happenings will come along but they are just temporary incidents, so treat them as such. Today will help you to get a clearer picture about life.

Blessed be. TttA.

IN THE STILLNESS OF THE MORNING!

Start your day with slow breathing and harmonious thoughts and you will find it will benefit you and your physical body greatly. Take time out but don't re-live yesterday. It is okay to keep the positive parts of what you have learnt for further help but take time to look at some of your old patterns of thinking, it's all too easy to fall into a pattern where you are always conforming to society. Unfortunately conformity can be like a flock of sheep without a shepherd or everyone wanting to be a leader and consequently things being pulled in all sorts of different ways. So prepare now, change is on its way, many areas will be sorted out and more will be done as you go along. It is okay to be practical but when something has outlived its use, get rid of it – somebody else could benefit from it. Don't try to do to much at once, little by little you will see what is to happen next and in the end you will see how big a difference it has all made to your feelings. Energy shifts are also occurring in you. After a year and a half of clearing, cleansing and renewing, some of it quite severe, it is finally starting to be beneficial to you. Start the New Year in a strong determined style and we will back you up as always. Enjoy today's sunshine and smile a bit more.

Blessings and love from us to you. TttA.

OPEN UP TO THE SOURCE FULLY!

Make sure you have an open mind and a good strong link to us so that when the storm rages you will only bend and not break. Clear your spiritual windows so that when you look through them you get a clear picture and at the same time, and at a moment's notice, you can tell that everything is in working order and functioning, it's just so much easier to make sure. We know that you know this stuff but you all need a reminder every now and then, just as you need 'turning over' to air the energy and to make sure that all the good energy's are in the right place to be of benefit to everyone. Some people need and want plenty, while others just require a top up, it all comes down to the many different levels of understanding and development that have been activated, you don't have to know them all, just what concerns you and yours. We have promised to take care of the others and we are in our own time, life's mysteries are not for everyone to solve, they are for learning from, one lesson at a time. We know well curiosity, reassurance and hopelessness, we all experienced them when we lived on Earth, they were and are just part of the school of life. You will find that later on it will be easier for you to peel away the outer crusts and see the core of the matter and because of that people will judge you and talk and wonder about you. Let them be – it's none of your business, just let today flow and get on with your day.

More tomorrow from the team. TttA.

KEEP YOUR HOME PEACEFUL!

Many will come to just sit in your home or in the beautiful garden but there is nothing you need to do, let them rest and bathe unrestricted, unhindered and unimpeded in the sunshine. The life force that will flow into their earthly bodies is healthy, wise and can be incredibly joyful. Stagnation and self-effacement is not for you or them and they will learn so much more. Your home is now our home as you promised us, so let it be so. From time to time we also need rest and to just be at times and your home is that sanctuary once again. We will make sure you are protected and well looked after. The birds and plants are showing a lot more energy this year and we have also noticed a change in your area, little by little things and situations are coming back into balance once again and because of this your system will be more manageable. So much has happened and yet there is so much more to come, but all in good time. Don't concern your self about that for now and don't try to work out a solution before it is ready to be discovered, today is today so go with the flow and just occasionally, rest by the riverside. It can be so different for different souls so remember the many different feelings and thoughts that you have had throughout your many lifetimes, we want you to understand that when you deal with others, you know what it can feel like. Rejoice when you know how much discipline and how much hard work is involved to go where you are going.

Blessings one hundred fold to you. TttA

PEACE BE UNTO YOUR VERY SOUL!

Let our peace stay with you and conquer whatever brings you to stopping and thinking. There may not always be a reason to stop but it should be done, try to take stock of things at least once a day, think about that. Do your best and we will do the rest, at present, time on earth is so very changeable and there are so many who are confused, but you don't need to be like all the others. It takes knowledge, stamina and courage to stay separate and to not be taken in by anything, you need to weigh things up carefully and ask yourself, where is this person coming from and what is their motive? Many do not know you as well as we do so ask us first and if in doubt just wait. To be patient and calm is not always easy but you are practicing everyday and that discipline is important so keep it going. Only by doing the lessons over and over again will your faith, love and trust multiply. You will start to see and hear more clearly and together with the way your recent overhaul is improving, you will be able to carry out your daily duties with a thankful heart and a willing spirit. Stop comparing, no one is ever the same, everyone has different lessons to learn so just let things be if they don't ask. Most of the time you do but it is still one of your lessons. Patience!

Blessed be. TttA.

PEACE ON EARTH!

Let situations and people be. If and when things need to alter or move we will let you know because we are in charge, remember how in the old days how we would let you and your followers know - well this universal law still applies in today's situations. You might think we are repeating ourselves but it's not just for any old reason, not when you can clearly see how it all does and is functioning. Try to imagine the Father's hand holding onto all the strings and doing what has been done for thousands of years for so many and go ahead with all the little things you have to do today. Sorting and sifting will make things clearer as to what is to stay and what has to go, including your spiritual life; concepts that are not accepted anymore, are old or not valid anymore all have to go. There is a fresh new interest in clarifying or understanding the truth; the passage of time and the many different translations have all distorted the truth and just added to the confusion so stand back and look at it all. Be silent and ponder what we mean, it's not easy but it is essential. Keep on working away as you are and know that we are close by. Be the captain of your ship.

Blessing to you all. TttA.

A MIRACLE DAY!

Yes my children miracles do happen and you are entitled to them, anything is possible so go forward and let the day unfold as it is meant to. Try not to make any big decisions just yet as there is so much in the melting pot and it's to soon to tell you everything. While you wait let us stay close together and enjoy the little things in life. Today you will get another reminder about spiritual law but first you need to withdraw and strengthen the ties with us. You outer circle should appear and if or when any ties need to be cut because you can't get through to us, tell us and we will do it for you. Last nights entities were very curious to see and hear what was going on at your place but you were well guarded so you were able to work undisturbed. So much depends on your energy input and output but none the less stay alert and listen carefully, the stillness of the morning will bring you what you want but remember to unwind in between situations. Just let things flow whenever possible and try to do some more of your forth and fifth dimensional artwork.

Blessings one hundred fold to you. TttA.

LEAVE THE OLD PATTERN BEHIND!

The old ways were learning times and while many lessons have taken a long time for you to accept and some positive ideas and beliefs were put aside, it was only because of the many negative things happening around you. Now that you understand so much more keep up your work, starting afresh next year and trust that we have every thing in hand. It will have a big impact in your life but in the meantime stay close and strengthen the bond between us, it has needed work for quite a long time, the string that holds us was nearly broken, but in time, once again, we saved you. Now there are stronger cords that have been put in place so that it will never happen again. Keep up the work on your spirit, your mind and your body. Look at the beauty of the many different flowers and the colours of the birds, they will all serve to uplift you and help you to see the many wonderful ways Mother Nature works. Don't try to work out any future happenings for now, things are going to be okay but there are some surprising events that are going to occur, there is a big year ahead for you so get ready for the work. You are going to experience many new connections that will bring exchanges and support so be patient and stay alert. Thank you for your obedience.

Eternal love to you. TttA.

TO KNOW IS NOT ALWAYS TO BE WISE!

Think about this. Knowledge can be very beneficial but watch out for its timing, when we say to wait you should, we know waiting can be hard for you, you get impatient at times but so do many others. Also, remember that while you might be ready the ones you are connected to may not be, so that's why you have to wait sometimes. Use the time to prepare and to recharge, waste nothing, not even time, use it to see and understand what is going on. Having confusion in your path is not good for you, stay clear of the muddlers and stirrers. Who are they anyway to disturb you when you are preparing for your next workload, for now solitude is a better friend for you. Don't listen too much to others and their moan and groans, you know what's going on with them so guard against those conditions. Trust, love and faith are still the best medicines for you. Next week will start to tell you a new 'story' but for now you will just have to wait, the future is not all that clear yet. In the meantime just handle today's work – you are still being tested. Your patience is holding up well at the moment, keep it up and you will succeed.

Blessed be. TttA.

RENEW AND RESTORE!

It is a big thing, but all you have to do is trust and give love with faith. Let go of negative interference and treat yourself as the honoured guest, don't overdo or under-do things. You are getting better at balancing things so stick with the pattern of believing and leaving things to us. Keep trying to get a better picture of things and the way they unfold in front of your very eyes, today is the first day of a new beginning so study hard and go with the flow, don't ask too many questions at this point. We call it 'being in the melting pot' and it is about becoming even more refined and pure. Remember you are not like other people because of this life-time's work on Earth, you are doing exactly what you were meant to do and soon the mists will clear and you will come to understand a great deal more. We know you can feel our presence and that you would like to see more, eventually that will come to pass. The season for giving is here now, but you gave out during the year and you will see more coming back next year. It is the waiting time for now but there is not long to go – patience my child of the light, we know you can do it.

Blessed be. TttA.

FINISH OF WHAT NEED'S TO BE DONE!

Clear your slate now for the end of the year so that when you start again in the New Year you start afresh. Pay up, give back or return things and say what you have to say, but remember to check what's called for before you say anything, afterwards you can relax and feel comfortable that you have done what was required of you especially when you look at the difference it makes. You will understand the reasons for it all if you remember the universal and spiritual laws, they are more important than the law of the land. Let go of any mysteries that you can't solve for now, it might just be too soon for a solution to them, so just wait. Carry on as normal, we are still behind you in your work so play more music and just let the day unfold as it may for you, tomorrow's happenings are not here yet, all in good time. Spend time outside in your garden whenever possible and try to enjoy life a little more. We know you are wondering about what is in store for you but as you know it is not clear yet, so stay calm and joyful and you will attract other like-minded people to you. It is possible after all this time to feel good and to be able to smile again. Cheering and loving thoughts from all of us, you are learning and getting better.

Blessings and health. TttA.

ADVICE AND GUIDELINES!

Many times we have given you just that and many times you have listened but not always understood and only seen a part of the picture, so some misinterpretation is what many people have received. That's all in the past now though as you are a lot clearer in yourself about the meaning of our love and teachings, we have waited quite a long time for that but in the mean time a lot has been cleared away. Still, there are a lot of little things that have to be done and finished off and once they are out of the way we can give you some more valid work to do and experience. Doing it this way you will always remember, its like in the old days when parables were used to explain the principles of how things worked. Now after years of studying and accepting what's been going on and after so many lessons with so many people, you finally know. Some will have come and stayed, others will have just passed by if they weren't ready. If they didn't stay it was because they couldn't feel comfortable and at ease or they had other shadows around them or even worse still, in charge of them. The signs will become clearer and more obvious, so take note. Keep on learning and trying to advance, you are getting ahead and you are getting a lot wiser.

Thank you. TttA.

MORE LIGHT!

We give you eternal light from the source in many folds this day, so let it brighten and cheer your day and environment and get into the very core of your soul. Enjoy the beauty of your lilies, whatever colour they are was given by me, your eternal Father and friend, the maker of all living things and the keeper of all that is beautiful. The practical side of life can be very helpful in these times of so many wanting so much, however if you do need help and you can't find and answer from your own experiences, all you have to do is ask me. The answer may not always be the way you expected things to unfold but it will come, in the right place and at the right time for higher self-development. You are clearing away so much at present which is great, it will leave room for new input, exchanges and good ideas from us, listen to our suggestions but just remember that they are not orders. Orders are not positive actions, the negative people that sometimes come to you use orders. At first they will try to tempt you, then eventually they will try to control you, however we will remind you so that you don't get drawn in by them, a signal will be given and you will begin to see and feel much faster who they really are. At our signal detach yourself from them at once and stay clear of the situation. Go on with your day now and enjoy it.

We wish blessings of health and wealth on you. TttA.

ONCE AGAIN WE MEET AND CONNECT!

Yes my child of the light, it's very good to know that when two or more of you gather in my name, that miracles will occur. Believe and gather as much truth about the universal spirit as possible and let us be in charge so that you don't have to do so much work, if necessary rest a little while by sitting at our well. The thing you are waiting for will happen, you will go on to do mighty work for the light in my name. You know that's so as you are one of our tools, just keep some balance in your life and remember to spread your work load out a bit more, don't concern yourself with the timing of it, things will be okay for all the important tasks. Back to priorities and order – lately you have looked at so many different areas of life and for you to take a stand with firmness is not easy, but you are getting there. Don't ask for instant results, they can occur but normally only when the quest is very urgent. These holidays you will experience a sense of peace, love and truth, so be as much as possible in a receptive mood to them. The time to prepare is here now, so prepare, this applies to your own body as well, its time to rejoice once again as it's a privilege to be renewed.

More tomorrow. Love TttA.

IGNITE YOUR SPIRITFLAME!

That's what we want you to do but a little 'flame' is not really enough, it needs to be burning brightly so that you are able to see what's going on and if things around you need igniting. The same also applies to when you light a candle, keep an eye on the flame and feel what's going on and what it is telling you to do, quite often we send you signals this way. At times you might think that not much is going on but actually there is, you can feel it, but as yet you just can't see it, your intuition is getting stronger but you need to keep practicing. As you do you will start to see improvements in other areas, believe and the thought will change things, be patient and you will see wonders unfold around you. To have a greater understanding of life and what it is all about can't be rushed or pushed, just keep doing what you are doing for now. We know how you feel and what you have been going through but it's been for a reason and soon that reason will bear fruit, leave it to us and just relax. The weekend will unfold to your liking so there is no need to fret, you are not the only one being attacked.

The more power you have the more likely you will experience interference, have courage my friend. TttA.

ONE DAY AT THE TIME!

Let us lead and guide you one day at a time. Don't concern yourself with the future just yet as no one knows exactly how or when. Most people that work for the light have different kinds of thoughts that normally don't belong in their lives and you are no different, but you need to discard those kinds of thoughts because they are unreal. You know by now what's what, maybe not entirely, but at least much more than before, you have risen above the worries of this world called Earth. There have been many tests to disrupt you and to put you off your goal, it's not been easy but you have done it. The worst tests have come from the ones close to you, they easily became a drain or just put their noses in where you didn't want them too, but that's all done with now. A clear communication line was called for and that's now sorted, there will still be challenges, some ongoing and some new, so keep an open mind and try to observe from a distance to see what's going on. When we say don't touch - don't, when that happens it is because the situation is too complex or too tangled for you to deal with. We are pleased that you are listening more and letting us know when you have seen something that needs our attention, long lost souls will return to you with a new outlook on things, observe but don't make any comment before you have talked with us.

Blessings and peace from us all, to you. TttA.

REVIVAL!

Remember to put new life into the old knowledge and long forgotten learnt lessons, for as you know nothing is really new. Most knowledge is only revived or 'dusted off' information that will become very useful for your future work, so use your time to collect as much information as possible and to practice what we have so often told you but remember to keep a balance about it all. Your special gifts will change enabling you to assist so many and to give them the information, from us, that they need to help them understand their life and the here after. Your training has been quite widespread because we wanted you have knowledge about a lot of different situations and backgrounds, but other people will have specialist knowledge. The school of life is so widespread with participants from all over the planet and we have made sure that it's well organised and that there are the right combinations to suit all areas. When you join up with other lightworkers support, listen and respect them and know that they will do the same to you. It won't really be you that they are listening to but us, and if and when others understand that, then that will be progress. Forever lasting growth and learning goes on and on and that is healthy.

Joy, love and health to you, from us. TttA

CLEAR THE PATH!

Today is an activation day and by the end of it you will see what went on during the connections. Conclusions and times of unfolding are now here, especially with so many questioning the truth of life and how things are working and now you will be able to tell them our version. The peace of your garden will aid and help you get things in balance, the sound of the birds and the water is a great benefit to you – you don't really need to be anywhere else, just ask and things will be done for you. Christmas this year will bring a different kind of joy with small and not so small surprises. We are working on restoring your inside parts, strengthening and renewing where it's needed. There has been a lot of wear and tear over the years however you will eventually be completely restored even better than before, so keep on doing your work and spreading the light around your environment. Next year you will have so many more come and sit and talk about eternity and life's lessons, so maintain the balance in your life and keep your patience and discipline in check, be thankful and give praise. Have a joyful and calm day and keep on working for the light.

Eternal blessings and love from your everlasting team. TttA.

TO KNOW IS ONE THING, TO BE WISE IS ANOTHER!

Quite often humans think they know what to do and when but don't you be too hasty, always ask first if it's wise for you to do what you intend doing or saying. To be able to apply wisdom yourself takes skill and patience, so be still and know that I am God the Father and will give you the right information to make a wise decision. Life at this time is full of different pressures and makes a certain number of people act out of the ordinary, it is the season of goodwill but don't give into the temptation of thinking you will receive. These things are best if they come with love from the heart and like most things it could be well meant but just not expressed in a clear way, communication therefore becomes very important – it is always a big part of your life, as is protection from undesirable quarters. There has been much growth this year in so many areas but next year we will teach you even more deeper and advanced truths. You will handle it well because of all the past years of training but let nature help you if necessary, your soul needs to be calm, tranquil and very wise. Trust is always a big part of faith and love, so take an instant longer to work on that area, you are getting better at it everyday, but keep your trust up.

Blessings and healing from us all. TttA.

ONCE UPON A TIME!

It sounds to you like an old story, but there is nothing old about anything, only situations that are being re-lived over and over again and hopefully slowly understood. People on earth learn faster when it comes to repetition and pictures; up and out here where we are, we mostly use telepathy, which is what we use to communicate to you with, for everyone's benefit. When you are relaxed and ready the answers always come faster and that's because of the way we communicate. We know how hard you are trying to change patterns that you have picked up from years ago and you are succeeding, just give a little bit more away – things that you don't need anymore. By doing that you will get rid of feelings and memories that no longer benefit you, a renewing and the chance to look at things again is best for you at the moment. Remember to cut off after the event though. Now back to the prime words "Once upon a time", it's how you will learn and never forget, it will make you stronger and help your trust and emotions stabilize. Just see the old year out and prepare for next year, everything happens in cycles, just like the universal patterns and life itself so you need to enjoy each day as it comes. Don't expect too much, that way you won't be disappointed, things happen to teach you lessons and to help you understand, remember there are still a lot of people out there that are asking and wondering.

Blessed be today and always. TttA.

GREETINGS!

Today will be a day of warm greetings and we will all rejoice with you at this time of giving, loving and peace. Some of you might not feel the love as yet but you are warming up to it, just know that before every change of importance there is always a time of preparation. Look at your garden as an example – before every growing season arrives it spends the season prior preparing for it. Most people that you come across are in need of nurturing and care in some way and while most of them will not admit it, the need is there. You will also experience a lot of goodwill this festive season, people will come to talk, while others will come to just sit, but whatever it is, it's not your concern. You have let us use your home and your garden and let us share in your lovely feelings so we use it all to send others to you. The purpose will always be the same – to enhance that person's growth wherever they are at and at whatever level they need help on. Your sanctuary and healing place will be used a lot more next year, like the climate, there are so many alterations and changes going on, especially in the soul and it is very confusing for many. Getting off to a healthy start each day means enjoying the stillness of the day at first light and the song of early birds. Do only a little at a time but focus on whatever it is that you are doing and all the other conditions will come right.

Blessings and joy from us to you. TttA.

GLAD TIDINGS!

Yes my friend, it is coming at last and the communication must improve. Some people in the past have not listened properly to you and to the message you gave them, their ignorance is great but all that will change gradually next year. We will also start to prepare the ground for your next conquest, be patient a little longer and you will start to notice the changes in people's attitudes and the weather patterns. For now though it is the season of goodwill, so take it into your heart and enjoy what comes your way. New connections will be activated and useful to the source but you need to be vigilant and aware, don't say or do too much for now. Everything in it's own time, leave it to us, leave your door open but put a guard by the entrance, if someone tries to enter, check, then let us know about it and what their purpose is. Some entities can be very subtle, while others can come as wolves in sheep's clothing - we know you know this but this is just a little reminder about people. Society is on the brink of a change at last and that's why we want you to open your eyes and to look and also to listen just that little bit more carefully. Traditions are fine just so long as you look at what they are doing for you.

Blessings and cheer to you all. TttA.

HEALING TO THE CENTRE
OF THE HUMAN HEART!

How easy it is, it just requires you to look under the surface and to clear it out. When you arrived on Earth everything had been dealt with and you started with a clean slate which is fine for a start but now you need to go all the way back to the very core, back to the beginning of your life on Earth. The many lessons you have learned on Earth have been quite revealing and in the long term basically rewarding. You might not see the rewards just yet as it's all still quite fresh but they will reveal themselves eventually. Unfortunately even though the New Year hasn't even started yet, the many questions are there. Also because all people have different ideas and hopes they therefore are wondering how life on this spirit plane is evolving. Big changes are afoot and even though so much has already altered it will still take a little time to get used to it. Your physical system is coming right, readying itself for the coming year. A different kind of work for the universe will be asked of you next year and that's why all the other areas had to be sorted out, so that you could start afresh. There aren't any situations that haven't been looked at or dealt with by us, however expect one more situation to be revealed to you tonight though. Let the spirit of Christmas be in you and flow out from you at this time.

Blessed be - we will be with you as always. TttA.

CARRY ON AS YOU HAVE STARTED!

Enjoy the season of goodwill, the good things and the little surprises. Let communication flow but remember to ask when to be silent or when to speak. Whether to listen or to speak depends on each situation and at which level the person is operating from, so if you don't ask you might strew golden grain on stony ground. You need to understand that many people keep things covered up and will only start to show their real feelings when they feel safe and secure. When a situation arises study it and learn from it. The life you have now is a study in itself on how one life can affect different souls and how you need to stay clear of negative things. Don't concern yourself with situations that only take energy and give nothing in return. Respect and listen to others and their ideas but don't take on board their ideas or thoughts if they aren't to your liking. Carry on with your bridging work but stay positive and calm. We always reach you that much easier when the conditions are right, when you have emptied out and today's meeting was a good example of a meeting that was of value, everything happened for a reason and we know you know, so tell others.

Greetings and love from us all. TttA.

OBSOLETE ONCE AGAIN!

Beware of interruptions, they always seem to come at the most unusual times but they happen to test you over and over again but don't despair though, it won't be forever. You are climbing the hill of faith, love and trust and while it has been a long road, don't give up now. If you slip occasionally, which would be only human to do, pick yourself up and go on. Over the last few days you knew that there had been a lot of interference and that was good. It was right not to write the last few days because you needed to be sure of what exactly was going on and who was telling you the story. Waiting is okay when it's called for, when you feel uneasy about something just leave it alone, this applies to many different situations. Time is eternal so let us decide. It's the same each morning when you wake and you surrender your will to us, when you let go of any misgivings you have and we in turn allow you some time to totally relax and to be stress free. Those moments of pleasure we give you, and allow you, at that time will relax and restore you before the new workload of the day comes in. At these times you will think that all work has ceased and while it has, it is also acting as a recharging and growing time. So enjoy the time, we have your situation in hand with the best possible human solution if you let us help you. Enjoy something every day and try to laugh a little more but speak your mind and stay firm. Believe in a positive outcome and it will happen. Thank you for trusting us so much more.

Blessings to you, from all of us. TttA.

BLESSED BE THIS DAY!

Remember my children how it all works and why you are here. Its good to know that you know and that you can keep an eye on your fellow man as many people can be sad, disturbed or low in spirit at this time of the year, with feelings and thoughts from years past welling up and rattling many of them. You have done well this year to see things for what they are, however remember the feelings from the many past Christmas celebrations. Keep the good ones and remember the lessons learnt from the not so good ones. The energies of city people and the environment are forever changing Christmas but all you can do is try to enter into the dimension of beauty, harmony and peace. Thankfulness is appropriate but also remember the good thoughts and things that have come your way. Stay positive and know that we are with you. Next year people will take a stand either for you or against you but don't worry about that for now. Let it all flow and you will be able to speak and do a lot of work for the light, communication will improve. Pay attention to the different energies around you, stay clear of any that make you feel uneasy and continue working on balance, joy and peace. We wish you all the best for the season and we thank you for writing most days. Amen.

May our star follow you. TttA.

REFLECTION TIME!

It would be wise to reflect a little at this time of the year, where you would like to be next year and to whom you want to give your energy and time to. Many other questions come to mind for us but you know what they are. Beware of so called friends, real friends won't push you around or try to obviously change your plans, people that listen to you now or give you respect will be in a much better space next year. Look at the patterns in the lives of the ones you are wary of, look at the expressions on their faces. Yesterday you received a good picture from us about the lives of some people, but don't worry, it was just a reminder that we felt you needed. To spend time with us is still beneficial and we needed to remind you why you are here. Keep on doing what you are doing until the end of the year, at that point we will tell you what we want next. People's attitudes are going to change, just as different nation's attitudes will, study the changes and you will learn much faster. Enjoy the rest of the day, a little surprise is in store for you, but first look after your spirit life.

Seasons blessings. TttA.

FREEDOM!

It's one of the most important things for humans and it gives them the opportunity to think and grow in the light and love, for the good of all mankind. That's a really big blessing and you should give thanks for it – count your blessings and see what you can do, not what you can't do. Every age has it's own blessings and teachings so don't get stuck in an era that isn't valid for you anymore, the past is the past and you should have learnt all the things that you needed then, to help you understand and grow. Carry on with your tasks, but try to be flexible and patient, we can't always stretch that far that we can help you straight away, but that's part of the learning curve for you for now. The freedom to be able to speak and communicate is important, as is free will, but you should know by now that to operate on that level you need to know the will of the Father. There are rules and laws wherever you go, however you need to study the universal laws and then you will be able to follow through with what you need to do. It's all very organized and the work involved is less but only when you understand how important every thought and action is. Many will try to tell you otherwise, they will try to tell you when or even if to listen but don't swallow anything they say before you have checked with us.

Love from us. TttA.

LET GO OF THE OLD AND ASK FOR NEW INPUT FROM THE SOURCE!

It's a tall order, but you would do well to ponder on that truth. All the old situations that were sorted throughout the year have to be left in the past now, otherwise you won't be able to get on with the new work that we are giving you. All is planned and all is good, so go bravely forward and trust that it is so. It's taken a long time to get as far as you have but work of importance can never be done in a hurry – all the looking in the dark corners and all the unfoldings can be very time consuming. Time is of the essence but don't panic, time is eternal and there is plenty of it to come for the evolvement. The speed that it happens is up to us, so surrender to it and let us get on with the planning. A good strategy is very valuable and its outcome will depend on how all the pieces alter and eventually fit where they are supposed to fit in the first place. Your mind will also help to 'blow' away old thought patterns. Just remember we can give you new input but first you must relax and empty out, otherwise nothing can be given. The old truths will always be solid and the law is our law.

Love and light from us all. TttA.

RENEW AND REJOICE!

Now at the end of the year you can afford to look back at what's been happening and where you made progress. Afterwards you can carry on as you have been but don't look back, it can be so easy to be apprehensive over old mistakes, but know that they were learning times. Look at life as a school and take time out when school is out. Too much discipline, too much of anything, doesn't always pays off so learn from all that has happened but don't be discouraged. We know that you wonder about many things but don't, we have it all in hand. Your future is a lot different to the others that you deal with, but that is how it should be. This mornings work was a chance for a good clean out before the year winds up and so that you can start afresh in the New Year, learning and working forever more with us. We have taken care of the bird spirit and now new life will come to you from another source, so keep busy but not too busy. The lesson to learn here is to keep a balance, no more "what if's". Trust, love and faith will get you through so don't be too hard on yourself. Not many would stay on as long as you have, especially when the times have been hard as they have been, but you have shown persistence and perseverance and that's fine but you need to keep up the exercise and work. As you get wiser and stronger it will get easier.

Love and support from us. TttA.

GOOD AFTERNOON!

Once again you have been disrupted but that's only to be expected at this time of the year, so don't worry, there are many that face constant disturbances and distortions, don't you get caught in that downward spiral, just concentrate and relax, you are being healed and looked after. Eternal time and Earth time are sometimes so far apart that it can be hard to judge sometimes. Beware of 'hangers on' and the 'misty' one – you know that one very well. Everyone should do their own homework and decide for themselves what, where and when, their spirit probably already knows, but unfortunately most people are controlled by their brain. That's society for you but that will change in the New Year and a more positive influx will appear. You might think 'at last', and you would be right to, there will be a lot of surprises for you to come and people will come back showing respect and consideration. Time wasting people will be fewer and more laughter will be heard. Your big clean out and sort out has left room for new input, but a little more room is still needed. A little bit at a time will be okay so just wait and don't try to work anything out just yet, that's our work.

Blessings and love from all of us. TttA.

ANOTHER YEAR HAS GONE!

Yes my children, it has been another year of learning, evolving and growing in spirit but please take the opportunities again next year to continue to grow. It will be a year of changes and clarification and love. Don't try to put a time frame on anything from us, it has to come naturally and at the right times, so carry on as you are with trust, love and faith, it's been a long time coming as we say, but once you have emptied out, you will receive. Make sure you don't carry over old burdens from last year or try to pick up what you have already discarded, as that would not be to your advantage. It's only natural to reminisce at times, but only let it be a picture that you can learn from, don't leave room for emotions as they will only cloud your judgement of any given situation. Today's trip was beneficial for you, you got to have another look at life and while you only got a few nice connections, its better than none at all. Don't concern yourself about people that don't listen, that's our job, let them fall by the wayside and go on with the other work that we have given you. There are many lessons still to be learnt and many situations still to be sorted out so tread carefully, especially around souls that have been wounded. Make sure that you don't take too much in but just in case, we'll continue to remind and support you.

Keep on your given tasks and lots of love and light. TttA.